D0515949

# Menú del Día

*More Than 100 Classic, Authentic Recipes From Across Spain*

## Rohan Daft

*Illustrations by* **Inés Vilaseca**

Simon & Schuster

NEW YORK    LONDON    TORONTO    SYDNEY

Simon & Schuster
1230 Avenue of the Americas
New York, NY 10020

Copyright © 2008 by Rohan Daft
Illustrations copyright © 2008 by Inés Vilaseca

All rights reserved, including the right to reproduce this book or
portions thereof in any form whatsoever. For information address
Simon & Schuster Subsidiary Rights Department,
1230 Avenue of the Americas, New York, NY 10020

First Simon & Schuster hardcover edition September 2008

SIMON & SCHUSTER and colophon are registered trademarks of Simon & Schuster, Inc.

For information about special discounts for bulk purchases,
please contact Simon & Schuster Special Sales at
1-800-456-6798 or business@simonandschuster.com

Designed by Jaime Putorti

Manufactured in the United States of America

10   9   8   7   6   5   4   3   2   1

Library of Congress Cataloging-in-Publication Data

Daft, Rohan.
Menú del día / Rohan Daft; illustrations by Inés
Vilaseca.
p.   cm.
1.   Cookery, Spanish. 2.   Food habits—Spain. 3.   Spain—Social life and customs.   I. Title.
2008001127
TX723.5.S7D327   2008
s641.5946—dc22

ISBN-13: 978-1-4165-4286-5
ISBN-10:    1-4165-4286-8

For Finlay and Felix

# Contents

# Segundos Platos 67

# Menú del Día

# INTRODUCTION

# The Menú del Día

*If the quality is there, there's no need to employ tricks in the kitchen.*

—SPANISH PROVERB

onday through Friday, come twelve noon or so, a freshly chalked blackboard will appear outside most restaurants in Spain. To start, it might typically offer *Espinacas a la Catalana* (spinach with raisins and pine nuts, the Catalan way), *Fideuà* (Valencian seafood noodles), *Remojón* (orange, salt cod, and potato salad from Andalusia), *Gazpacho* (cold tomato, green pepper, and cucumber soup), or *Lentejas* (lentils stewed with onion, bacon, and sausages).

To follow, *Marmitako* (the thick red Basque tuna broth), *Bacalao a la Llauna* (baked salt cod with tomato, *pimentón*, and white wine), *Fricandó* (braised shank of beef with any available wild mushroom), *Lomo a la Malagueña* (pork loin roasted with sweet Málaga wine, almonds, and raisins), or *Chilindrón* (Navarran lamb with red pepper sauce).

Dessert (*postre*) is always a simpler, more concise affair: *Flan* (caramel custard) often suffices and, always, a plain yogurt and whichever fruit was good and to be had for a decent price at the market that morning.

To drink, it's beer, a glass or more of the house red, or water, and finally, coffee.

And as decreed by the Franco government in 1965 to provide a good, cheap, solid lunch for the workers and something more than the sun for tourists and their all-important cash, all of this is to be had for a price a good deal less than that if the dishes

were ordered individually. This is the *Menú del Día*, a very Spanish institution and home to Spain's classic, favorite dishes.

There survives a proud tradition in Spain—formed partly, at least, by the dictates and memories of some hard times past—of making the most of what you have; of respecting food as much as enjoying it; of eating locally and with the seasons; and of never allowing any imposed thrift to get in the way of flavor. There still exist a great number of small, family-run restaurants where what goes on the menu depends on what is good at the local market in the morning. And much of what there is at the local market remains local produce.

The Spanish of all classes and backgrounds pay great reverence to their home-produced delicacies such as *jamón ibérico de bellota* (ham from acorn-fed pigs), *percebes* (gooseneck barnacles), *lechazo* (milk-fed baby lamb), and *azafrán* (saffron), but no more than they do to their many types of beans and their chickpeas and lentils, their pork belly and sausages and their sardines.

These are the ingredients and dishes that have always stood Spain in good stead and there is sentiment as much as there is tradition attached to them: *Paella* still only appears on *Menús del Día* on Thursdays, the day that rice was distributed during the long-gone days of rationing.

The law that obliged restaurants to offer the *Menú del Día* disappeared with Franco in 1975 (and not all of the restaurants mentioned in this book offer one, so you might want to check beforehand), but its inherent appeal endures. Lunch remains the big meal of the day in Spain, a country—perhaps the only remaining country in the world—that still finds time to all but close down for three hours to properly enjoy it. In fact, a 2006 survey found that 63 percent of working Spaniards still sit down to the *Menú del Día* every weekday.

This book is the result of the time I have spent living, writing, traveling, and more importantly, shopping in food markets and specialty stores: cooking, watching other people cook, and eating in Spain. And in particular, it is the result of a wonderfully revelatory, meandering, and—save for a brief list of regional products and dishes and the names of a few recommended restaurants—unplanned

ISLAS BALEARES

Fornells
Mahón
Palma de Mallorca
Ibiza

La Coruña
Santiago de Compostela
Vigo
Pontevedra
Lugo
Oviedo
Santander
San Sebastián
Bilbao
Vitoria
Pamplona
Burgos
Valladolid
Zamora
Segovia
Zaragoza
Girona
Barcelona
Tarragona
Salamanca
Madrid
Cuenca
Cáceres
Toledo
Castellón
Valencia
Badajoz
Albacete
Alicante
Murcia
Sevilla
Córdoba
Jaén
Huelva
Jerez
Jerez
Granada
Málaga
Almería
Cádiz
Algeciras
Tarifa

ISLAS CANARIAS

Santa Cruz de Tenerife
Las Palmas de Gran Canaria

four-month-long journey I undertook in 2007. Made by train, bus, and thumbed lifts, this journey ended up crisscrossing pretty much the whole of Spain and rewarded me with all sorts of anecdotes, information, and recipes from, among others, chefs, restaurateurs, market stall holders, olive oil producers, mushroom hunters (professional and amateur), fishermen, farmers, and foragers. No one I met refused me help.

While I hope the recipes contained here are both appealing and delicious, I hope equally that, along with the accompanying introductions and notes, they give you as much of an insight into Spain and the Spanish as they do their eating habits.

These recipes will serve you well for brunch, lunch, or dinner, all year round. Fresh ingredients feature prominently and so do bold flavors. And when it comes to the cleaning up, you will further praise the great Spanish tradition of one-pot cooking. This is good, solid food and the odd slip, miscalculation, or change of ingredient is unlikely to spoil your enjoyment of it. There are certainly some dos and don'ts, some basic practices and techniques, but this is not and never has been a precise, persnickety cuisine and to treat it that way would be to lose its essence. None of these dishes is complicated and a number of them you will be able to put together in minutes. However, others will require some of your time—that most treasured and closely guarded (if not noble) of Spanish commodities.

Something of Spain's relationship with time was explained to me one evening shortly before Christmas 2002 in the restaurant car of the sleeper train from Barcelona to Paris when, over steak and Rioja, an immaculate, blue-suited, and white-bearded eighty-six-year-old Valencian told me why he wouldn't be following his family—children, grandchildren, great-grandchildren—to live in France. He loved them dearly, and he missed them as much. "There's no time to do nothing in France," he said, earnestly. "Not in France, Germany, America, England . . . But in Spain . . . in Spain there's still time to do nothing."

Some Spanish Implements,
Ingredients, Preparations,
and Tips

n alphabetical order:

## Artichokes

The leaves of a good, fresh artichoke will be tightly packed and perfectly green.

To prepare artichokes for dishes such as *Alcachofas a la Montilla* (Artichokes with Montilla-Moriles Wine, page 60), first break off the coarse outer leaves. Remove the stalk and trim the base with a sharp knife until it is relatively smooth and rounded (or leave a half-inch-long protrusion of stalk, if you prefer). Rub the cut area with lemon juice to prevent blackening. Cut off the tough tips of the remaining leaves and rub the exposed ends with lemon juice. The artichokes can now be sliced and sautéed, boiled whole, or treated in whichever way you like.

If the artichokes are very young and fresh, the wispy choke that covers the heart is perfectly edible. If you prefer to remove it from older, tougher artichokes, do so after they are cooked by plucking out the inner cone of leaves with your fingers and then carefully scraping it away from the heart with a knife. Replace the cone of inner leaves before serving. Alternatively, if you are slicing the artichokes before cooking, simply trim away the choke with a sharp knife.

You can prevent staining your fingers brown when preparing artichokes by wearing rubber gloves.

In Catalonia, artichokes are commonly roasted whole or cut in half lengthwise and cooked over charcoal. They are eaten with grilled meats, *butifarra* sausage (see page 72), and dressings and sauces such as *Romesco* (page 56) and

*Allioli* (page 154), with the resultant pile of gnawed blackened leaves and left-over bones forming a centerpiece for the table.

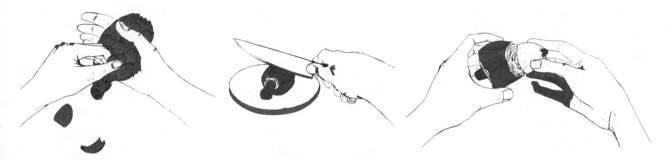

1. Break off coarse outer leaves.  2. Remove stalk and tips of leaves and trim base.  3. Rub cut areas with lemon.

## Avocados

You can help avocados to ripen by wrapping them in newspaper.

## Bacalao

See Salt Cod.

## Bananas

Some people in the Canary Islands ripen bananas by wrapping them in a blanket. Others use brown paper bags.

## Beans and Pulses

Dried beans need to be soaked overnight before cooking. Different types of beans take different times to cook and may take more or less time depending on how old they are, so you will need some experience cooking dried beans before you can absolutely master such dishes as *Alubias Blancas con Almejas*

(White Beans with Clams, page 104) and *Tolosanas* (Red Beans with Pork Rib, Chorizo, Bacon, and Blood Sausage, page 120). You can cook lentils straight from dried.

## Cazuelas

*Cazuelas* are shallow glazed earthenware casseroles—an indispensable item in the Spanish kitchen. They can be used on a gas stove, in the oven, or under the broiler (but not, alas, on an electric stovetop). They retain and spread heat perfectly, they come in every size, are easy to clean and not expensive; they can lend an authentically rustic appearance to your table. Season your *cazuela* before use by soaking it in water overnight. Then fill it with water and place over a low flame until the water has almost all evaporated (see illustration, page 55). Wash it after each use in warm water, without soap. A well-looked-after *cazuela* should last for approximately three years. See Resources (page 159) if you can't find one locally.

## Chestnuts

For how to peel chestnuts, see *Jarrete con Castañas* (Beef Shank with Chestnuts, page 86).

## Chorizo

*Chorizos* are pork sausages flavored with various amounts of sweet or spicy *pimentón* and sometimes garlic, pepper, oregano, thyme, or chile. Spain's national sausage, they are produced everywhere except—traditionally, at least—the *Paises Catalanes* of Catalonia, Valencia, and the Balearic Islands. Flavorings aside, they vary with regard to their size, whether they are fresh or cured (and if so, for how long), and, to a lesser degree, the breed of pig the pork comes from.

Harder, longer-cured *chorizos* are generally sliced and eaten as they are, but are also used to flavor stewed dishes such as Lentils (page 22). Those that are shorter cured and softer are either eaten in their natural state or cooked. And fresh *chorizos* are commonly added to stews such as the *Cocido* (page 74) and, famously, fried with eggs (page 73).

The fattest, pinkest *chorizo* is named after the place it comes from, Pamplona, and is the closest Spain gets to an Italian salami. In Asturias, *chorizos* tend to be a touch spicier, short-cured and soft, and are sometimes cooked in cider or flaming spirits such as the grappa-like *aruja*. A *chorizo gallego* (Galician) will be small, soft, and smoked. A *chorizo* from La Rioja will contain large globules of fat, be a rich red in color, have a soft but slightly crumbly texture, and, if it comes from the Iberian breed of pig, might just be the best of them all.

## Cuttlefish

See Squid.

## Fruit and Vegetables in General

The end of the stalks and stems of fruits and vegetables give a good idea of how long ago they were cut or picked. Look for something fresh and sappy, not black and dry.

Test the freshness of melons and pineapples by holding the top in the palm of one hand and the bottom in the palm of the other and pressing gently; the tops and bottoms are always the first parts of these fruits to show signs of deterioration.

Always wash soft fruit such as strawberries and raspberries with their stems on so they avoid taking on water.

Green vegetables will retain their color better when boiled if you do not place a lid on the pan.

## Frying

To dust smaller fish or cuts of fish or meat with flour before frying, place them in a zipper-top plastic bag, add the amount of flour required, seal the top of the bag, and shake rigorously.

See "Olive Oil" below for information on frying with olive oil.

## Garlic

For a milder, more rounded flavor, remove the green germ from the center of garlic cloves before use.

It is easier to peel a clove of garlic if you first crush it lightly with the blade of a knife.

## Greens

Washing greens such as chard and collards in hot water can remove a certain bitterness from their flavor.

## Ham

Though the word *serrano* traditionally refers to a small V-shaped cut made at the knuckle of a ham to remove part of the fat, it has now become a generic term for cured Spanish ham. The very best cured Spanish ham, however, is *jamón ibérico*, with *ibérico* referring to Spain's native black pigs (*jamón serrano* is made from the less-revered white pig). And the best *jamón ibérico* is labeled "*de bellota*," which connotes that the animal has been raised outdoors and fed on a high percentage of acorns. If you are after the very best Spanish cured ham, simply look for the words "*jamón ibérico de bellota*" and ignore terms such as Jabugo (a town where they produce some excellent *jamón ibérico de bellota*, but also a fair proportion of serrano), *pata negra* (while the *ibérico* breed of pig that produces *jamón ibérico* does famously have black feet, so do other breeds), and *reserva* or *gran reserva* (which mean whatever the producer wants them to mean). The laws are changing for ham imports, so there will be more available in the United States.

Prosciutto may be used as a substitute for *serrano*.

Cooked or boiled ham is known as *jamón dulce* (sweet ham) or *jamón de York*.

## Olive Oil

Though a lot of terminology and general bunkum is applied to Spanish olive oil, in reality it's a relatively straightforward subject. Basically, there are three types: that which is mechanically cold-pressed from the olives and consumed without further ado ("extra virgin" and "virgin"); that which is mechanically cold-pressed and then "refined" and blended with extra virgin or virgin oils to make it palatable ("olive oil"); and that which is extracted from the pomace or pulp of the olives that produced the extra virgin and virgin oils and then, again, blended with extra virgin or virgin oil ("olive pomace oil" or *oruja*). The difference between extra virgin and virgin is the level of oleic acid (not more than 1 percent for extra virgin and not more than 2 percent for virgin), a monounsaturated fat that helps to reduce cholesterol and—contrary to popular belief—does not affect the taste of olive oil. Some labels will also tell you if the oil is of a single variety (*picual, arbequina, gordal,* etc.) or a blend, and if it has *denominación de origen* (a Spanish-government-recognized producing area) status. Some twenty-five varieties of olive exist in Spain and *arbequina* (fruity, light), *cornicabra* (medium fruit, often blended), *hojiblanca* (fresh, sweet), and *picual* (spicier) are those olive varieties that produce most of the oil. Extra virgin oils are the most expensive and are best (and generally only) used for dressings and sauces as they have a fuller flavor and can turn bitter with heat. The refined oils (olive oil, olive pomace oil, or *oruja*) are better for frying because they are best suited to high temperatures.

If you're going to reuse olive oil that has been used for cooking, do not mix it with clean oil.

## Onions

The Spanish claim you can avoid tears when chopping onions by dipping the blade of the knife in water as you go.

## Paellas

With regard to *paella* pans, it is best to wash them in water only and lightly oil them with olive oil after use. When you make *paella*, do not fill the pan to a level above the rivets that attach the handles.

With regard to *paella* the dish, cover it with a newspaper and let it stand for ten minutes off the heat before serving. This works particularly well if you're making a drier style of *paella* (see *Paella de Marisco*, page 37) and want your rice *a punto* (firm to bite) and the grains separate, as opposed to softer and soupier. And, if for no other reason, it's more than worth doing just for the moment when, on removing the newspaper, the aroma hits you. Do not use aluminum foil or a pot cover: your *paella* will be dripped on.

## Pimentón and Dried Peppers

*Pimentón* is Spanish paprika (which you should feel free to use if you do not have access to the real thing) and an absolute staple in the Spanish kitchen. It's made from ground dried red peppers, and the best example is said to come from the valley of La Vera in the westerly inland region of Extremadura, where they lightly smoke the peppers over holm oak (the tree that provides the acorns for the Iberian pigs) before grinding them. There are both sweet and spicy *pimentones*, with the former being more commonplace. *Pimentón* is used as much as a colorant as a spice and, as you will discover from a good many of the recipes on the following pages, it is much more commonly used in the cooking process than as a garnish. That said, fried eggs are far from averse to a light dusting of it.

The Spanish also make great use of whole, unground, dried red peppers (does anyone dry green peppers?). The principal varieties (and the varieties that you will encounter in this book) are *ñoras* which are much used in Catalonia (see *Sofrit Pagés*, page 98), and the larger, slightly less spicy *choriceros* or *pimientas de salsa* from the Basque country (see *Bacalao a la Vizcaína*, page 114). Dried peppers are either chopped finely or reconstituted (boil them for approximately twenty minutes and then gently scrape the flesh off the insides of the skins—see *Cordero en Chilindrón*, page 100) before being used in sauces or dressings (see *Romesco*, page 56) and thickening and flavoring *picadas* (again, see *Sofrit Pagés*, page 98).

## Peas

Test the freshness of peas in the pod by rolling a bunch of them (the pods, not the peas) between your hands. The more they squeak, the fresher they are.

## Rice

In Spain, it is said that 1 kilo (2.2 pounds) of rice will feed seven people. See *Paella de Marisco* (Shellfish Paella, page 37), *Paella Mixta* (Mixed Paella, page 40), *Paella de Verduras* (Vegetable Paella, page 42), and *Arroz a Banda* (Rice with Poached Fish, page 68) for cooking with rice. Use Spanish Bomba or Senia rice for these dishes. Arborio or short-grain rice will work, but your results will be better with the real thing.

## Saffron

The strength of different types and harvests of saffron vary widely, so it is advisable to start with a small amount and add to it if and when desired.

The flavor of threads of saffron can be intensified by lightly toasting them in a dry frying pan or wrapping them in aluminum foil and quickly heating it over a flame or in the oven.

The best saffron is said to come from the villages of Barax, Munera, and El Bonillo in Castile–La Mancha.

# Salt

The wholly natural sea salt from the *salinas* (salt flats) of the Balearic Islands, the southern Mediterranean coast, and the vicinity of Cádiz on the Atlantic is best. Use any sea salt if you do not have access to it. Table salt will suffice.

# Salt Cod

Remove the salt from salt cod (*bacalao*) and prepare it for cooking by soaking it in cold water for as long as your fishmonger or the package instructions tell you, changing the water three or four times in the process. To check that it is properly desalted, use a pair of tweezers to remove a tiny piece of the raw flesh from the center of the fish and taste it.

You can treat desalted salt cod in pretty much the same way that you would any fresh fish.

It is traditional to break desalted salt cod by hand, as opposed to cutting it with a knife.

Salt cod is also very good eaten desalted and raw (see *Remojón*, page 58, and *Xató*, page 56).

# Shellfish

Fishmongers tend not to appreciate it, but the Spanish habit of tapping shellfish with a finger to see if it moves is the best way of finding out how fresh it is.

Fresh shrimp with slightly black markings on the head are not necessarily a bad thing; it probably means that they haven't been salted to preserve them.

Place clams in lightly salted fresh water for half an hour or so before cooking to clean them of sand.

# Squid

Cleaning squid is a much easier job than it appears. Simply pull on the head until it comes away from the body. Reserve the tentacles and discard the rest (except the ink sac if you are preparing the Black Rice on page 52). Pull the plastic-like cartilage out of the body of the squid and carefully rinse away the gluey white stuff inside. Or ask your fishmonger to do it for you.

Remove any sand from the tentacles of the squid by rolling them between your hands when washing.

# Stocks

The success of many of your *paellas* and *fideuàs*—as well as a good number of sauces, soups, stews, and braises—will depend as much on the quality of your stock as that of your principal ingredients. For real depth of flavor with your fish stock, use as best a mixture of fish that you can. Good Spanish fishmongers will always have a big pile of *pescaditos de roca* ("little fish from the rocks"—a motley selection that might include tiny gurnard, flat fish, rouget, monkfish, and, if you're lucky, body-giving scorpionfish) available. If you can, add a chunk of a nice cartilaginous monkfish head, too. And if there are some on hand, add a few mussels, little crabs and/or shrimp heads. For meat, poultry, or game stocks, simply replace the fish with the same amount or more (by weight) of carcasses or bones. For a fish stock recipe, see page 18.

For a vegetable stock, see *Paella de Verduras* (Vegetable Paella, page 42).

# Tomatoes

Skinning and seeding tomatoes is a tiresome process. Simply cut them in half and use a coarse grater to take the flesh off the skin. Then, if desired, sieve to remove the seeds.

# Fish Stock

1½ pounds mixed fish and shellfish
5 cups water
1 medium onion, halved and with the peel left on
1 or 2 cloves garlic, unpeeled
1 stalk of celery (optional)
1 or 2 sprigs parsley
Sea salt

MAKES 3 ½ CUPS

Put everything in a large pot. Bring to a rolling boil and remove any gray foam that forms on the surface. Reduce to a simmer. Let it bubble gently for about 45 minutes, until the water has reduced by about a third. Strain without worrying about missing a few bits and pieces; they will only add flavor.

VARIATION: For a red, slightly sweeter stock, add 2 or 3 halved ripe tomatoes.

*Don't overcook fish stock—it can turn a touch bitter. Seal the stock (plastic water bottles work well) and refrigerate; it will keep well for three days. Shake or stir well before use.*

# 2

## Primeros Platos

(STARTERS)

Fideuà ❧ Lentejas ❧ Salmorejo ❧ Setas con Huevo Pochado ❧ Escalivada ❧
Lombarda Rehogada ❧ Judías Verdes con Pimientos Rojos y Jamón Serrano ❧
Piperrada ❧ Pimientos con Pasas y Almendras ❧ Ajo Blanco ❧ Ensalada de Habas
al Perfume de Apio ❧ Pimientos Estofados ❧ Gazpacho ❧ Ensalada de Tomate
Murciana ❧ Paella de Marisco ❧ Paella Mixta ❧ Paella de Verduras ❧ Ensalada de
Patatas, Mejillones, y Chorizo ❧ Ensalada Mixta ❧ Patatas con Chorizo ❧ Menestra
Riojana ❧ Espinacas y Garbanzos ❧ Espinacas a la Catalana ❧ Arroz Negro ❧
Sopa de Ostra Estilo Pontevedra ❧ Sopa de Ajo ❧ Xató ❧ Remojón ❧ Alcachofas a
la Montilla ❧ Caldo Gallego ❧ Alboronía ❧ Gazpachuelo

# Fideuà

## SEAFOOD NOODLES

1 large or 2 small cuttlefish or squid (about ¾ pound)

5 tablespoons olive oil

6 cloves garlic, unpeeled

10 ounces *fideos*, vermicelli, or broken-up spaghetti

1 small yellow or white onion

5 ripe tomatoes

2 rounded teaspoons hot or sweet *pimentón* or paprika, or a mixture

Salt

3 cups Fish Stock (page 18)

**SERVES FOUR TO SIX**

Fideuà *is a specialty of Valencia. The story goes that a fisherman out at sea once forgot the rice for the* paella *and so made do with some* fideos *(tiny crooked sticks of pasta) that he had to hand. While many a good dish has undoubtedly been stumbled upon in such a make-do way, it's more likely that a little more thought went into* fideuà, *as the Moors first introduced pasta to Spain in the ninth century.*

*Whatever its origins, it's a wonderful dish, and particularly so if you like garlic. Don't stint by failing to place it under the broiler for a couple of minutes to finish it off; that the top crisps and bristles like a hedgehog adds a nice contrast of texture and suggestion of warm toast to the flavor as much as it does a pleasing appearance.*

*The Spanish traditionally eat their pasta well done, and* fideuà *is no exception. A good* fideuà *needs to be prepared with a full-flavored stock. Eat it with* Allioli *(page 154).*

*As in Italy, pasta is traditionally served as a starter in Spain. That said,* fideuà *is also a very popular main course for Sunday lunch.*

Clean the cuttlefish and cut the body into small pieces about 1 inch square and the tentacles to lengths of 1 inch.

Gently heat 3 tablespoons of the olive oil in a large (about 12-inch diameter) paella pan, *cazuela*, or frying pan. Add the garlic and cook over medium heat for 3 to 5 minutes, until golden. Add the *fideos*, stirring them so they are well coated in the oil. Cook for 5 minutes, stirring continuously, until they turn a light golden brown. Remove the *fideos* from the pan and set aside. Remove the cloves of garlic from the *fideos* by spearing them with a knife; set them aside.

Add the remaining tablespoons olive oil to the pan and fry the cuttlefish for approximately 10 minutes, or until it crisps slightly at the edges.

While the cuttlefish is cooking, peel and medium-chop or coarsely grate the onion and skin the tomatoes (see page 17). Coarsely grate 4 of the cooked cloves of garlic. (You do not need the other two garlic cloves.)

Remove the cuttlefish from the pan and set aside. Add the onion to the pan, stirring well. Add the tomatoes, grated garlic, the *pimentón*, and a pinch of salt. Stir well.

While the mixture is reducing and thickening, heat the stock.

Add the *fideos* to the pan and stir well to coat with the tomato mixture. Add the cuttlefish, stir well, and spread the *fideos* evenly across the pan. Pour over the hot stock so it just covers the *fideos*. Cook over medium heat for 10 minutes, until the *fideos* have absorbed the stock and are perfectly soft; add more stock if you need to.

Remove from the heat and place under a hot broiler for approximately 3 minutes, or until the *fideos* bristle. Leave to stand for 5 minutes before serving.

**NOTE:** This recipe comes from the Rosselló family in Palamós on Catalonia's Costa Brava. Palamós is also home to an exceptionally good *lonja* (fish auction), at the adjacent public market, which is where *los Rosselló* buy their fish and shellfish, all of it straight off the boat that day. In Spain, unlike some countries, fishermen are enthusiastic fish eaters, and the no-frills cafés and bars-cum-restaurants next to the *lonjas* are invariably the places to find the best, freshest fish, prepared in the simplest, most complimentary way.

# Lentejas
## LENTILS

3 tablespoons olive oil

1 medium yellow or white onion, chopped medium

1 medium red or green bell pepper, chopped medium

1 medium carrot, chopped medium

6 ounces bacon, chopped into $1/2$-inch pieces

2 cloves garlic, chopped

2 tomatoes, chopped

1 $3/4$ cups lentils

2 ounces *chorizo*, chopped into 1-inch pieces

2 ounces *morcilla* (blood sausage), chopped into 1-inch pieces (optional)

1 bay leaf

$1/2$ teaspoon cumin seed, crushed in a mortar

1 sprig thyme

1 rounded tablespoon of parsley, chopped

1 medium potato, peeled and cut into $1^{1}/2$-inch chunks

4 eggs

**SERVES FOUR**

*An ample, ages-old stew, inspired by thrift and—as is generally the case with such dishes—held dear to the Spanish heart. This is a dish for using up whatever there is to be used up—knob ends of* chorizos, *ham bones, stray* morcilla *(blood sausage), the scraps of yesterday's roast. There is no "classic" recipe so feel free to improvise. Lentils are always an excellent standby dish as you can cook them straight from dried and they'll soak up all the flavor of whatever you have to cook them with. If you can, use the Spanish caste-llana variety which are large, greeny brown, and turn slightly floury in the cooking.*

*In westerly, landlocked Extremadura, which borders Portugal and shares certain of its culinary practices, they sometimes put eggs to poach on top of the lentils in the pan. Each serving then arrives at the table topped with its own egg, the yolk of which is promptly punctured to run free. A few crystals of sea salt make for the perfect finishing touch.*

Heat the olive oil in a large pan with a lid. Cook the onion, pepper, and carrot over low heat, stirring well. When the onion begins to soften, add the bacon and garlic. Cook 10 minutes more and add the tomatoes. Cook for 10 minutes, stirring well.

Rinse the lentils under cold running water and remove any stones. Add the lentils to the pan, coating them well in the tomato mixture. Add 2 cups of water and stir well. Add the *chorizo* and *morcilla*. Add the bay leaf, cumin, thyme, parsley, and potato. Add another 2 cups of water and stir well. Raise up the heat, then reduce to a simmer.

Cook for about 25 minutes, checking to see if you need to add more water.

Just before the lentils are done, place 4 eggs to poach on top of them and place the lid on the pan.

Remove the bay leaf and thyme sprig. Serve the eggs on top of the lentils.

**VARIATION:** For an easy summer lentil salad, follow the instructions above but leave out the meat and poached eggs. Leave to cool and dress with olive oil and sea salt to taste. This works well with a firmer, French *Puy*-style lentil and is particularly good served with hard-boiled eggs.

# Salmorejo

## COLD TOMATO AND BREAD SOUP WITH HAM AND EGG

2 pounds ripe, flavorful
    tomatoes
1/2 cup fresh breadcrumbs
2 cloves garlic
Sea salt
6 tablespoons extra virgin
    olive oil (*picual*, see page
    14, or something spicy is
    best)
1 1/2 tablespoons sherry or
    white wine vinegar
4 hard-boiled quail eggs or
    2 hard-boiled hen eggs
1/2 cup diced cured ham,
    such as *serrano* or
    prosciutto

**SERVES FOUR**

*In southern Spain, Juan Peña is a proud man. His Mesón Juan Peña in Córdoba is celebrated nationally for the quality of its traditional dishes, and none more so than the brilliantly light and flavorful salmorejo, or rather the twenty-something varieties of it that he has now come up with. Salmorejo is a tomato soup of Andaluz origin that is thickened by bread (more often than not a weighty white country bread that here they call telera), lifted with a good dash of a local peppery picual olive oil and wine vinegar (Juan uses a Montilla-Moriles from the famed, twinned wine-making towns of Montilla and Moriles, some fifteen miles south of Córdoba), and decorated with a sprinkling of chopped egg and diced cured ham. Juan's great salmorejo experiment has seen him supplant the tomato and introduce the likes of beets, red and green bell peppers, hazelnuts, and olives. In 2007 the leading young Michelin-starred experimentalist Dani García cited him as a major influence in a very complimentary piece (which Juan says he has absolutely no interest in reading) in the newspaper El Mundo. But, for all that, the traditional salmorejo very much remains the most popular choice at Mesón Juan Peña and, with sincere thanks to Juan, here's the recipe.*

Chop the tomatoes and puree them in a blender or food processor with the breadcrumbs, garlic, and 1 teaspoon salt until you have a completely smooth mixture. Slowly and thoroughly mix in the olive oil and vinegar. Chill in the fridge.

Add more oil, vinegar, and salt to taste. Serve topped with diced hard-boiled egg and ham.

**NOTE:** Juan stresses that it is very important to not skin or seed the tomatoes.

# Setas con Huevo Pochado

## MUSHROOMS WITH POACHED EGG

*It is more common in Spain to stir eggs into sautéed mushrooms and scramble them (what is called a* revuelto, *and famously made with shrimp and asparagus) than it is to poach them and put them on top. But this is the way that they do it at the wonderful Hartza in Pamplona (see Lamb with Red Peppers, page 100) with springtime's* perrechicos *mushrooms—tiny, white, and almost hazelnut-like. You can use any mushrooms that are available. While button mushrooms are good, cremini are better, and if you can get a mixture of wild mushrooms, this will be sublime. Smother them with egg yolk and sprinkle with a little salt before eating.*

1 pound mushrooms
3 tablespoons butter, unsalted or extra virgin olive oil
4 eggs
Sea salt

**SERVES FOUR**

Brush and/or wipe the mushrooms clean with a damp cloth. Trim the bottom of the stems. If you are using small mushrooms (up to approximately $1^{1}/_{2}$ inches in height and with caps of a similar diameter) and the stems are tender enough to eat, leave them whole. Otherwise, separate the caps from the stems. Heat the butter over low heat in a large frying pan. Add the mushrooms (including the stems if you are using them) and sauté them for approximately 8 minutes, until they have softened and warmed through.

Meanwhile, poach the eggs. Carefully drain the eggs to remove all water. Divide the mushrooms between four plates and top each with a poached egg and salt to taste. Just before serving, break the egg yolk to smother the mushrooms.

**NOTE:** Add a little finely chopped onion, garlic, and parsley if you are using button mushrooms or others that you fear might be lacking in flavor.

# Escalivada

ROASTED AND MARINATED RED PEPPERS, EGGPLANT, AND ONION

2 medium yellow or white
   onions, unpeeled
2 medium eggplants
4 red bell peppers
2 heaping tablespoons
   soaked and bite-size
   pieces salt cod (optional)
2 cloves garlic, finely
   chopped
Sea salt
Black pepper
2 tablespoons white wine
   vinegar
1½ cups extra virgin olive
   oil

**SERVES FOUR**

*The vegetables for this favorite Catalonian dish are traditionally roasted in the embers of a wood fire, which, naturally, gives them a smoky flavor. Barbecue grills (and escalivada goes very well with barbecued meat and fish) do the job equally well. Otherwise, a conventional oven will suffice. Escalivada benefits from being left to stand overnight in the fridge. The optional salt cod adds a complementary and pleasantly chewy touch of salt; alternatively, try serving it alongside canned or bottled anchovies. Black pepper is not a classic* escalivada *ingredient and not everyone uses vinegar but they work very well.*

Preheat the oven to 350°F. Wrap the onions in aluminum foil and roast them on a baking sheet for 20 minutes. Add the eggplants and peppers and roast for 30 minutes more, turning once or twice, until they are perfectly soft. Remove the onions, eggplants, and peppers from the oven and set aside to cool.

Seed the peppers and cut them and the eggplants into strips of ½ inch or so. Skin the onions and cut them into ¼-inch rings. Place the eggplants, peppers, and onions in a single layer in a rimmed serving or baking dish. Sprinkle with the salt cod, if using. Sprinkle with the garlic. Add a pinch of salt (a small one if you are using salt cod) and a couple of twists of black pepper. Sprinkle with the white wine vinegar. Pour on the virgin olive oil to almost cover the vegetables and, preferably, leave to stand in the fridge overnight or for a few hours at least before serving.

# Lombarda Rehogada

## RED CABBAGE WITH PINE NUTS AND GREEN APPLE

*This is typical of the central plain, and a very good accompaniment to roasts and game, especially the red-legged partridge common to La Mancha—a dish that is best prepared with a spicier extra virgin olive oil such as a* lucio *or* picual *(see page 13).*

Lightly toast the pine nuts by rolling them around in a dry frying pan over a low heat for approximately 3 minutes. Set aside.

Core and medium-chop or slice the cabbage and boil in salted water for 3 minutes, until tender but not mushy. Drain well.

Peel, core, and slice the apples to a thickness of approximately $^1/_4$ inch.

Heat the olive oil over medium-low heat in the frying pan in which you toasted the pine nuts. Add the apple and cook for approximately 3 minutes, until it begins to brown, turning it in the oil as you go. Add the garlic to the apple, stir well and cook for 2 minutes more. Add the cabbage, mixing it well with the apple and garlic. Add the pine nuts, a pinch of salt to taste, mix well, and serve.

1 rounded tablespoon pine nuts

1 medium head red cabbage

2 green apples

4 tablespoons extra virgin olive oil

2 cloves garlic, finely chopped

Sea salt

**SERVES FOUR**

# Judías Verdes con Pimientos Rojos y Jamón Serrano

## RUNNER BEANS WITH RED PEPPERS AND CURED HAM

2 medium red bell peppers
1¹⁄₂ pounds green beans
3 tablespoons olive oil
2 cloves garlic, finely
   chopped
2 ounces chopped *serrano*
   ham or any cured ham
   such as prosciutto, cut
   into small cubes or strips
1 tablespoon chopped
   parsley
Sea salt

**SERVES FOUR**

*In Castile-León they use this full-flavored recipe to prepare those plentiful, slightly flabby late-season green beans that are more prone to bend than snap. Any tired green vegetable will respond well to the same treatment, as will younger, stronger leaves such as spinach, mustard greens, and collards.*

Preheat the oven to 350°F and bring a large pot of salted water to a boil.

Roast the red peppers on a baking sheet for approximately 25 minutes, until they are slightly charred and their skins have loosened. Set aside to cool.

In the meantime, remove the top and tail and the strings from the beans and cook in the boiling water for approximately 5 minutes, until they are tender but not mushy. Drain and set aside.

Skin and seed the peppers and cut them into strips the same width as the beans.

Heat the olive oil over medium heat in a large, deep frying pan. Add the beans and the garlic, stirring well. After approximately 2 minutes, add the peppers, again stirring well. Cook for 2 minutes, then add the ham, parsley, and a pinch of salt. Stir well, turn off the heat, and cover for 5 minutes before serving.

# *Piperrada*

## RED PEPPERS, ONION, AND TOMATO WITH FRIED EGGS

*A pan-Basque dish, this is as common to the French part of that land (as Basque nationalists have it) as it is to the Spanish. Some scramble the eggs, but the most successful examples fry them slowly on top of the cooked peppers, onion, and tomato, basting with the slightly sweet and smoky oil. Pipe-rrada is best eaten with a couple of slices of everyday* serrano *ham and bread to wipe up the last of the egg and oil. It is not essential to skin the peppers but it does improve the flavor.*

4 medium red bell peppers
2 medium yellow or white onions, sliced
1/4 cup olive oil
3 cloves garlic, finely chopped
2 sprigs thyme, oregano, or marjoram (or 1 teaspoon dried)
3 medium tomatoes, skinned and seeded (see page 17)
Sea salt
8 eggs

**SERVES FOUR**

Preheat the oven to 350°F. Roast the peppers on a baking sheet for approximately 25 minutes, until they are slightly charred and their skins have loosened. Set aside to cool.

In the meantime, cook the onions in the olive oil over low heat for approximately 25 minutes, until they are soft but not brown.

Skin, seed, and slice the peppers into strips. Add the peppers, garlic, and herbs to the onions and cook for 15 minutes, stirring well.

Stir the tomatoes into the onions and peppers. Raise the heat to medium-low and cook for 5 minutes more until the tomato has reduced and thickened. Add salt to taste. Carefully break the eggs over the onion, pepper, and tomato mixture and baste them until they are done.

**NOTES:** If you find you do not have sufficient oil to baste the eggs, you can always finish them under the broiler.

If you want to prepare an eight-egg *piperrada* but do not have a frying pan large enough, make two smaller versions by splitting the onion, pepper, and tomato mixture in half and frying the eggs in batches of four. You can also prepare this with four eggs, one per person, for a lighter dish.

# Pimientos con Pasas y Almendras

## RED PEPPERS WITH RAISINS AND ALMONDS

4 large red bell peppers
2 tablespoons blanched
  almonds
2 tablespoons raisins (fat
  Málaga raisins, if you
  can)
Boiling water
2 tablespoons extra virgin
  olive oil
Sea salt

**SERVES FOUR**

*A meeting of the Arabic (almonds and raisins) and the New World (peppers, which arrived from South America), this dish comes from Andalusia and it's very good with roast chicken (stuffed with garlic and, perhaps, with a well-salted half lemon), pork, or more mature lamb. The almonds should be distinguishable and add a crunch so don't grind them to dust; you can use whole toasted pine nuts if you prefer.*

Preheat the oven to 350°F. Roast the peppers on a baking sheet for approximately 25 minutes, until they are slightly charred and their skins loose. Set aside to cool.

Lightly toast the almonds over low heat in a large dry frying pan. Transfer them to a mortar and gently crush them (you do not want a powder), or roughly chop them with a knife.

Put the raisins to soak in boiling water. Skin the peppers and cut them into strips.

Heat the olive oil over medium-low heat in the pan in which you toasted the almonds. Add the peppers. Strain the raisins and add them to the peppers. Stir well and heat through for 5 minutes. Add salt to taste. Stir in the crushed almonds, stir well, and serve.

# Ajo Blanco
## COLD ALMOND AND GARLIC SOUP WITH GRAPES

*An Andalusian summer soup of almond milk made sharp with garlic and sweetened by grapes. That this dish has survived since Roman times will tell you how good it is. The consistency should be that of low-fat milk. Though it is seemingly obligatory for photographs of* ajo blanco *to feature half grapes floating, island-like, on top, you will find that in reality this is a hopeless task to execute.*

⌒

Soak the breadcrumbs in 3 tablespoons of water. Mash the garlic in a mortar with a pinch of salt. Squeeze as much water as you can out of the breadcrumbs and mix them into the garlic and salt. Place in a blender with the almonds. Work to a smooth paste. Add the olive oil, tablespoon by tablespoon. Add the vinegar. Add ice-cold water until you have the desired consistency. Place in the fridge to chill.

Add more vinegar and salt if desired and serve in small bowls or glasses with three or four grape halves.

2 ounces fresh breadcrumbs (approximately 4 small slices, crusts removed)
2 cloves garlic, peeled
Sea salt
3⁄4 cup blanched almonds
3⁄4 cup extra virgin olive oil
1 tablespoon sherry vinegar
1 quart ice-cold water
8 grapes (muscatel preferably), peeled and seeded if you can be bothered

**SERVES FOUR**

# Ensalada de Habas al Perfume de Apio

## BROAD BEAN AND CELERY SALAD

2 pounds (unshelled weight) baby broad beans or fresh fava beans
1 stalk celery
1/2 medium, sweet yellow or white onion, finely chopped
1 tablespoon capers (salted or in vinegar), rinsed and dried
2 tablespoons extra virgin olive oil (or to taste)
2 teaspoons white wine vinegar (or to taste)
Sea salt

**SERVES FOUR**

*As he has every morning at eight forty-five (Sundays aside) for the last thirty-eight years, Isidre Gironés starts his day at Barcelona's mesmerizing 500-stall La Boquería market. Every day brings something special. And Isidre is there to sniff it out—quite literally, sometimes—for his restaurant Ca l'Isidre, a cozy, family-run affair in the tiniest of nondescript streets that is patronized by all—the King and Queen of Spain and the king of the Spanish modernist chefs, Ferran Adrià, among them—who appreciate that the best food starts with the best ingredients. If it's March, it's the six-ounce langoustine that come in from Arenys de Mar, half an hour up the coast. April means morels from the woods in the foothills of the Pyrenees. The tiny, sharp, new-season broad beans that Isidre uses in this salad arrive at the Fruitas Teresa stall in January and come from Prat de Llobregat just to the south of Barcelona.*

Bring a pot of water to a boil and prepare a bowl of ice water. Shell the broad beans (there is no need to peel them) and plunge them into the boiling water for 15 seconds. Drain and plunge into ice water so they retain their color. Drain again and leave to cool.

Wash, trim, and remove the tough outer skin and strings from the celery stalk with a potato peeler. Cut the celery stalk into approximately 24 matchstick-shaped pieces by cutting it into four equal size lengths and then cutting each length into three pieces. Then cut each piece in half again, lengthwise. Take the broad beans and spread in a single layer on a large plate or platter and sprinkle with the celery. Then sprinkle with the onion and capers. Dribble on the olive oil and the vinegar, and salt to taste.

*Salads are not generally prepared with dressings or vinaigrettes in Spain. The most common practice—in most restaurants—is to pour on oil and then vinegar to taste, followed by a pinch or two of salt.*

*You wouldn't know it from the guide books but there are some forty markets in Barcelona besides La Boquería. Of particular interest are Galvany, which is the most upscale, and Sant Antoni, which is almost as big as the Boquería but, minus the tourists and all the chopped-fruit-in-plastic-cup stalls that cater to them, rather more authentic.*

# Pimientos Estofados

## STEWED PEPPERS

6 medium red or green
  bell peppers, or mixed
  peppers
3 tablespoons olive oil,
  preferably a *picual* or
  something peppery
1 small yellow, red, or
  white onion, chopped
2 cloves garlic, finely
  chopped
2 sprigs fresh thyme or
  1 teaspoon dried
1 rounded tablespoon
  chopped parsley or 1
  rounded teaspoon dried
Red or white wine or sherry
  vinegar
Sea salt

**SERVES FOUR**

*Peppers—stewed in a harsher, more peppery olive oil with garlic, parsley, and thyme and finished at the table with a splash of aged wine vinegar and a scattering of sea salt—go deliciously with both fatty meats and oily fish. The variety and color of the pepper or peppers is up to you, but a predominantly red mixture will have more bite. This dish is enjoyed throughout Spain, but is said to have originated in La Mancha.*

Preheat the oven to 350°F. Roast the peppers on a baking sheet for approximately 20 minutes, turning once, to loosen their skins. Remove from the oven and leave to cool.

Gently heat the olive oil in a frying pan. Add the onion to the pan, stirring well. Cook over very low heat for approximately 15 minutes, stirring regularly, until onion is soft but not browned.

In the meantime, skin and seed the peppers and cut them into strips approximately $1/2$ inch wide. Set aside.

Add the garlic to the onion, stirring well. Add the thyme, and stir in the parsley. Add the peppers and cook very slowly, stirring regularly, for approximately 20 minutes.

Drain off any excess oil. Add vinegar and salt (in that order) to taste at the table.

# Gazpacho

## COLD TOMATO, GREEN PEPPER, AND CUCUMBER SOUP

*Surely a close second to Paella (pages 37 to 43) as Spain's most famous dish, Gazpacho is of Andaluz origin and was nothing more than an unexciting, field workers' muddy-looking, bread-thickened vegetable soup until the arrival of tomatoes from the New World transformed it into the altogether lighter, more vibrant dish of today.*

*The essence of Gazpacho is that it is fresh, and to that end it is imperative that all the ingredients (save for the breadcrumbs) are just that. Some Gazpachos will incorporate ingredients such as red pepper, lemon, and cumin, but the following recipe is for what is considered to be the classic version. Some prefer to leave the vegetables unpeeled. You can use a mortar and pestle to prepare it, but a food processor or blender is certainly a lot easier.*

*Gazpacho is sometimes served with a garnish of finely chopped cucumber, tomato, green pepper, onion, hard-boiled egg, and croutons.*

2¹⁄2 pounds ripe tomatoes
2 cloves garlic, peeled
Sea salt
2 ounces breadcrumbs (approximately 4 slices day-old bread, crusts removed)
1 medium green bell pepper
1 medium cucumber
¹⁄2 cup extra virgin olive oil
1¹⁄2 tablespoons sherry vinegar
¹⁄2 cup ice water

**SERVES FOUR**

Skin the tomatoes (see page 17). Mash the garlic in a mortar with a good pinch of salt. Put the breadcrumbs to soak in a little cold water. Seed the pepper and cut into six strips. Peel the cucumber and cut into large chunks. Squeeze as much water as you can out of the breadcrumbs, add to the mortar, and combine with the garlic and salt. Place the breadcrumbs, garlic, and tomatoes in the food processor or blender and work together until you have a puree. Add the pepper and cucumber and continue until all is amalgamated and smooth. Gradually, tablespoon by tablespoon, add the olive oil. Add the vinegar. Add the ice water little by little, until you have the desired consistency. Taste and add more vinegar and/or salt if needed. Place in the fridge to chill before serving.

**NOTE:** Do not ever be tempted to add ice cubes to *Gazpacho* to chill it; you will only succeed in diluting it.

# Ensalada de Tomate Murciana

## MURCIAN TOMATO SALAD

1 clove garlic, peeled

Sea salt

1/2 teaspoon cumin seeds, plus a pinch for garnish

Squeeze of fresh lemon juice

1 tablespoon sherry vinegar

1/2 cup extra virgin olive oil

10 good, ripe medium tomatoes

1 rounded tablespoon chopped parsley (optional)

**SERVES FOUR**

*The region of Murcia, bunched between Valencia and Andalusia and with its easterly border the Mediterranean, produces stunningly good fruit and vegetables. This is one of the ways that the people enjoy their tomatoes, making good use of two other very local ingredients: cumin and lemon.*

Make a vinaigrette by pounding the garlic, a pinch of salt, and the cumin in a mortar, and then adding the lemon juice, sherry vinegar, and olive oil. Add the flesh of 3 of the tomatoes (see page 17). Stir well and adjust the seasoning to taste.

Roughly chop the remaining tomatoes into six or eight pieces each and place, skin side down, on a flat dish. Pour over the tomato vinaigrette and sprinkle with a few cumin seeds, the chopped parsley, if using, and sea salt to taste.

# Paella de Marisco

## SHELLFISH PAELLA

Can Salinas is a simple, block-built roadside place, tables all outside under a dozen or so olive trees. It overlooks the salt flats just outside Ibiza Town. The menu features half a dozen paellas and a Fideuà (page 20), nothing more, but a better paella or fideuà you'll be hard pushed to find. Owner and chef Manuel Ribes is from Valencia, the home of paella, and paella has been his business for some thirty years.

Paella was originally a basic, land-workers' dish, prepared outside in the rice fields over open fires of—preferably—orange or olive wood, and served for lunch. It's a method of cooking rice as much as it is a dish, and endless variations abound, two particularly delicious ones being hare and artichoke, and salt cod and cauliflower.

While an authentic Valencian paella will feature—as it would have a couple of hundred years ago—small pieces of rabbit, a handful of snails, a few butter beans, three or four green beans, and a lot of saffron-yellow rice, the more contemporary, commonplace paella can by contrast appear almost vulgar with its altogether richer, more luxurious ingredients of shrimp, lobster, langoustine, clams, and chicken. Indeed, as any true paella aficionado will tell you, for all the fancy ingredients with which you can dress up a paella, the rice always has been and always will be the star element. And for

1 small yellow or white onion, chopped
3 tablespoons olive oil
2 cloves garlic, chopped
2 ripe tomatoes, skinned and seeded (see page 17)
1 teaspoon sweet *pimentón* or paprika
1⁄2 teaspoon hot *pimentón* or paprika (optional)
6 threads saffron
41⁄4 cups Fish Stock (page 18)
21⁄2 cups short-grain rice, preferably Spanish Bomba
16 clams
16 mussels
8 large shrimp or 1 lobster, prepared as for *Caldereta de Llagosta* (see page 123)

**SERVES FOUR TO SIX**

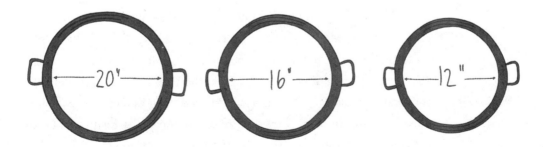

*(continued on next page)*

*many, the very best bit of the rice is the* soccarat, *the thin crust, faintly caramel sweet and chewy, that forms on the base of the pan in the cooking. Many
a Spaniard will dismiss as substandard any* paella *that comes without soccarat.*

*This Paella de Marisco is very simple and very good. The rice is firm
and just a touch chewy, and the bottom should reward you with a good
scraping of* soccarat. *Adjust the amounts of* pimentón *and saffron to taste
and use half a cup of stock less if, like me, you prefer your rice drier. And
to finish, cover it with a newspaper and let it stand for ten minutes off the
heat before serving.*

*You will need a large* paella *pan,* cazuela, *or frying pan: 18 to 22 inches
diameter is the ideal size, but 14 inches will just about suffice.*

Place your pan over low heat and slowly cook the onion in the olive oil.
When the onion has softened considerably but not browned, add the
garlic. Stir well and cook for 3 minutes. Add the tomatoes and stir well.
Add the sweet *pimentón* and hot *pimentón* (or double one or the other if
you prefer). Stir well. Add the saffron (you can lightly toast the saffron
beforehand in a dry frying pan to intensify its flavor, if you choose).
Raise the heat to medium and stir well.

Heat the stock separately until simmering.

Add the clams, mussels, and shrimp to the pan and stir well to
coat with the mixture. After 2 minutes, remove half of the shellfish, set
aside, and add the hot stock to the pan. Bring the stock to a simmer.
Add the rice, spreading it evenly across the pan. Arrange the shellfish
you have set aside on top. Cook over medium-low heat for 25 minutes—moving the pan every 5 minutes to spread the heat—until the
stock has all but evaporated and the rice is beginning to stick to the

bottom of the pan (you can check this with a wooden spatula or spoon). Turn off the heat and cover with a newspaper. Leave for 10 minutes.

Remove the newspaper, take in aroma and serve. *Paella* is traditionally eaten warm, not piping hot.

**NOTE:** *Paella* is more usually featured as a starter on Spanish *Menús* (in the same way that pasta is in Italy) and for that reason it is included as a starter here. That said, it is also served as a traditional Sunday lunch main course.

*It is important to ensure that the heat is spread evenly when preparing a paella. In Spain, there exist extremely useful diffusing gas-ring contraptions that plug into the stovetop or a propane tank. If you can't find one (see Resources, page 159), it is extremely important that you gently move the pan around over the heat as you go. Alternatively, try cooking your* paella *on the barbecue or, in the original way, outdoors over an open fire.*

# Paella Mixta

## MIXED PAELLA

6 threads saffron

1/4 cup olive oil

Half a small chicken or rabbit, approximately 2 pounds, cut into 2-inch pieces

4 pork spareribs or country-style ribs, cut into 1-inch pieces

1/2 medium white onion, chopped

1/2 red bell pepper, chopped

1/2 green bell pepper, chopped

1/4 pound flat green beans, cut into 1 1/2-inch lengths

2 cloves garlic, finely chopped

2 tomatoes, skinned and seeded (see page 17)

1/2 teaspoon sweet *pimentón* or paprika

1/4 cup fresh or frozen shelled peas

8 large shrimp or langoustines, shell on

8 mussels or clams, scrubbed

2 1/2 cups short-grain rice, preferably Spanish Bomba

4 1/4 cups chicken stock or water, heated

Sea salt

**SERVES FOUR TO SIX**

Paella Mixta *is what you could now safely call a standard* paella *(and what certain Spaniards call tourists'* paella*) and is so named because it incorporates both shellfish and chicken or rabbit, and perhaps a few pieces of pork rib. That said, there really is no set way of preparing it, so feel free to vary the ingredients; squid and* chorizo *sometimes appear, as does cubed* magro de cerdo, *which is lean pork. Do bear in mind, however, that the dominant ingredient of an authentic* paella *is always the rice. With regard to the pan, it should really be at least 18 inches diameter and preferably larger (though you can just about get away with something of 14 inches). Some very serious Valencian and Murcian* paellas *are prepared with the rice in one layer, with not one grain encroaching on another.*

Lightly toast the saffron in a large dry paella pan or frying pan over low heat for approximately 10 seconds. Remove and set aside.

Pour the olive oil into the pan, raise the heat to medium, and add the chicken and pork. Cook for 15 minutes, or until lightly browned, stirring well. Remove the chicken and pork rib from the pan and set aside.

Add the onion, red and green peppers, and green beans and cook for approximately 10 minutes, stirring well, until soft but not brown.

Add the garlic. Add the tomatoes, saffron, and *pimentón*, stir well, and cook for 5 minutes more, stirring well.

Add the peas. Stir the chicken, shrimp, and mussels into the vegetable mixture. Cook for 5 minutes, then remove half of the shrimp and mussels and set aside. Add the rice to the pan, stir it well and spread it evenly across the pan. Gently pour over the stock. Add salt to taste. Place the shrimp and mussels that you set aside on top of the *paella* and cook for approximately 15 minutes, until the rice is the texture that you want and the stock has considerably reduced. Remove from the heat and cover with a newspaper for 10 minutes before serving.

**NOTE:** See *Paella de Marisco* (Shellfish Paella, page 37) for general tips on preparing a *paella*.

*There are two camps with regards to paella and onion, with one of them arguing vociferously that the dish should never include it. The choice is yours.*

*There are also two camps with regards to paella and stock or water. Stock will give a fuller flavor but can smother the taste of more delicate ingredients, such as shellfish. Again, the choice is yours. Sometimes, the stock is added to the pan before the rice. And sometimes, it can be the other way around. Use whichever method you prefer.*

# Paella de Verduras

## VEGETABLE PAELLA

### For the stock

2 chicken carcasses, chopped

1 veal knucklebone (optional)

1 stalk celery, stringed and finely chopped

1 medium leek, cleaned and finely chopped

1 medium carrot, finely chopped

1 small yellow or white onion, finely chopped

2 quarts water

### For the paella

2 spears green asparagus

¼ medium red bell pepper

¼ medium green bell pepper

2 snowpea pods

2 thin green beans (*haricots verts*)

1 small yellow or white onion

4 artichoke hearts (see page 8)

1 ounce yellow *trompetes* or other wild mushrooms

1 ounce green or white cauliflower

½ carrot

¼ cup olive oil

2 cloves garlic, finely chopped

2 ounces peas

1 ounce baby broad beans

*The recipe below is for a* Paella de Verduras *that I prepared one January lunchtime in the kitchen of Ca l'Isidre in Barcelona, under the tutelage of owner Isidre Gironés (who has inherited his Valencian mother's expert touch for cooking with rice) and his head chef, Jordi Juan. As the ingredients were selected that morning in Barcelona's Boquería market, it is possible that you will not have immediate access to all of them, particularly the yellow* trompetes *mushrooms and garrofón beans. Do not fear; simply use the same quantity of whatever you think will work best from what is available to you, bearing in mind that freshness—and hence taste—is important and a variety of colors and textures add interest. Do that and—in spirit at least—your* Paella de Verduras *will be no less authentic than Ca l'Isidre's. For your information, the only difference of opinion with regard to our ingredients came when Jordi said no to Isidre's suggestion of a few mustard leaves.*

Place all the stock ingredients in a large stockpot, bring to a boil, and simmer for 1½ hours, skimming off any foam that forms on top. Strain and refrigerate until needed.

Preheat the oven to 400°F. Medium-chop the asparagus, peppers, snowpeas, green beans, onion, artichokes, mushrooms, cauliflower, and carrot (each spear of asparagus cuts into approximately eight pieces, the peppers into ½-inch strips and each strip into approximately six pieces, and the rest to a corresponding size) and set them aside, keeping them separate.

Heat the olive oil in a paella pan or large frying pan 18 to 22 inches diameter (14 inches diameter will *just* do if you have nothing larger) over medium-low heat. Add the garlic, onion, and red and green peppers. Stir well and cook for 5 minutes.

Add the rest of the vegetables (except for the *ganxet* and *garrofón* beans) and the saffron. Stir well and cook for five minutes.

Add 4¹/₂ cups of stock, the *ganxet* and *garrofón* beans, and a pinch of salt. Stir well and cook for 2 minutes.

Add the rice, spreading it evenly across the pan. Cook for 5 minutes.

Remove from the heat and place in the oven for 15 minutes, or until the stock has been absorbed by the rice. Leave to stand at room temperature for 5 minutes before serving.

**NOTE:** Isidre does not cover his paella with newspaper (see *Paella de Marisco*, page 38). For more recipes from Ca l'Isidre see Broad Bean and Celery Salad (page 32) and *Crema Catalana* (page 138).

3 tablespoons tomatoes, skinned and seeded (see page 17) or canned chopped tomatoes

2 to 6 threads saffron (if you are not using top quality saffron from Castile–La Mancha—see page 15—you will need 6)

1 ounce fresh *ganxet* beans, or fresh or frozen borlotti or lima beans

1 ounce *garrofón* beans, or lima beans

Sea salt

2¹/₂ cups short-grain rice, preferably Spanish Bomba

**SERVES FOUR TO SIX**

# Ensalada de Patatas, Mejillones, y Chorizo

## WARM POTATO, MUSSEL, AND CHORIZO SALAD

2 pounds mussels

1¹⁄₂ pounds potatoes, unpeeled

1 medium yellow or white onion, chopped medium

6 tablespoons olive oil

1 clove garlic, chopped

¹⁄₂ cup dry white wine

1 bay leaf

¹⁄₂ cup Fish Stock (see page 18), or water

Sea salt

Squeeze of lemon

1 tablespoon white wine or sherry vinegar

1 hard-boiled egg

1 tablespoon chopped fresh parsley

¹⁄₄ pound *chorizo* (see page 10), or cooked pork sausage or chopped bacon

**SERVES FOUR**

*Galicia's myriad brooks and rivers run into the sea by way of the* rias, *huge fjords that have long provided the perfect habitat for scallops, clams, cockles, oysters, octopus, mussels, and more. This is a satisfying warm dish: mussels steamed in wine and stock, potatoes to soak up the resultant broth, and fried chorizo to give a crunch and suggestion of spice. It comes from the enchantingly Tolkienesque sounding and pretty town of O Grove, which looks over the Ria de Arousa, Spain's premier source of mussels.*

Bring a pot of salted water to a boil. Debeard the mussels and scrub them clean with a stiff brush or steel wool.

Peel the potatoes, slice them thickly, and boil them until tender. Drain and set aside.

Cook the onion slowly for 10 minutes, stirring regularly, in 2 tablespoons of the olive oil in a lidded pan large enough to hold the mussels. Add the garlic. Cook for another 5 minutes, or until both the onion and garlic are soft but not brown. Add the wine and raise the heat until it bubbles. Add the bay leaf and the stock. When the mixture is bubbling, add the mussels, stir well, and cover.

When all the mussels have opened (about 3 minutes), remove them from the pan, retaining the liquid in which they have cooked. Leave the mussels to cool.

Make a vinaigrette in a salad bowl with a pinch of salt, a squeeze of lemon, the vinegar, and 3 tablespoons of olive oil. Chop the egg and add to the vinaigrette. Add the chopped parsley. Mix in ¹⁄₂ cup of the liquid that the mussels cooked in. Add the potatoes.

Take the mussels out of their shells and add to the potatoes. Mix well.

Chop the *chorizo* into rounds approximately $1/2$ inch thick and fry in 1 tablespoon of olive oil over medium-high heat for 2 minutes, until they crisp. Sprinkle the *chorizo* over the top of the potatoes and mussels and spoon over a little of the oil in which it was cooked. Add salt to taste.

**NOTE:** You can use any *chorizo* but the soft-cured variety that is commonly known as *casero* (homemade) will work best. Alternatively, use any coarse-cut sausage or a slice or two of chopped bacon or lardons.

# Ensalada Mixta

## MIXED SALAD

1 head iceberg lettuce
2 medium tomatoes
½ red bell pepper
 (optional)
1 medium sweet yellow or
 white onion, peeled
4 spears canned or jarred
 white asparagus
1 small (3-ounce) can tuna
2 hard-boiled eggs
2 anchovy fillets, rinsed
 and patted dry
16 green olives
Extra virgin olive oil
Red or white wine vinegar
Sea salt

**SERVES FOUR**

*The ubiquitous* Ensalada Mixta *is much maligned, more because of the inability of so many Spanish restaurants to produce a salad in any other way, rather than anything to do with the dish itself, which is actually quite good (particularly if you are new to it). The Spanish tend not to make dressings for their salad, preferring instead to dribble on oil and vinegar and sprinkle a pinch or two of salt to taste. Add more anchovies if you choose; half a fillet per person is what you generally get with a standard* ensalada mixta *but as you may discover, that is hardly satisfactory.*

Cut or tear the lettuce into pieces of approximately 3 inches square and wash and dry. Wash and slice the tomatoes. Wash and slice the red pepper into four rings. Thinly slice the onion. Drain the asparagus and tuna. Peel the hard-boiled eggs and cut them in half. Rinse the anchovy fillets under cold running water and pat dry.

Spread the lettuce evenly across a large platter. Arrange the other ingredients artfully on top with the tuna in the middle. Dribble on olive oil and vinegar and sprinkle salt to taste. Transfer to individual serving plates without tossing.

*Txokos are traditionally male Basque gastronomic societies that date back one hundred years or so; perhaps they originated from trade associations. They celebrate traditional Basque cuisine and sometimes particular ingredients (such as Álava potatoes on the next page and the beans of Tolosa, page 120). Membership in a txoko involves male bonding through eating, drinking, singing, and playing cards.*

# Patatas con Chorizo
## POTATOES WITH CHORIZO

*Here is a simple example of how* chorizo *is commonly used to give flavor rather than substance to a dish.* Patatas con Chorizo *is popular throughout Spain; this version comes from the Alavés province of the Basque Country home of the firm and white Álava potato, a tuber so prized it has its own txoko (or fan club, see opposite page). This is an especially good dish if you can resist the pull of your can of powdered* pimentón *or* paprika *and use instead the flesh of a couple of reconstituted dried red peppers (see page 14).*

～

Peel the potatoes and either cut or "break" them (see *Marmitako*, page 110) into pieces of the size that you would for roasting. Gently heat the olive oil in a deep frying pan. Add the onion to the pan. Stir well and cook over low heat for 10 minutes. Add the garlic to the onion, stirring well again. Cook for 5 minutes more, or until the onion and garlic are soft but not browned.

Add the potatoes and stir again to coat them in the oil and onion mixture. Chop and add the *chorizo*, the flesh of the peppers, and the bay leaf. Stir well to amalgamate and cover with boiling water. Simmer for 30 minutes, or until the liquid has all but disappeared.

Remove the bay leaf. Sprinkle with chopped parsley and salt to taste and serve.

**VARIATION:** *Patatas viudas* (widowed potatoes) is so called because it's *Patatas con Chorizo* minus the *chorizo*. It's an ages-old dish, and very good with grilled or roast pork, lamb, or chicken. Substitute the chorizo in the recipe above with one rounded teaspoon of *pimentón* and a table-spoonful of olive oil.

2 pounds white potatoes
3 tablespoons olive oil
1 medium yellow or white onion, chopped
2 cloves garlic, chopped
¼ pound soft-cured *chorizo*, coarse pork sausage, or chopped bacon
2 dried *choricero* red peppers or any mild dried red peppers (reconstituted) or 1 heaping teaspoon sweet *pimentón* or paprika
1 bay leaf
Boiling water
1 tablespoon chopped parsley
Sea salt

**SERVES FOUR**

# Menestra Riojana
## SPRING VEGETABLES WITH OLIVE OIL

½ pound chard
½ pound unshelled peas
½ pound unshelled broad
  beans
½ pound green beans,
  chopped into 1-inch
  pieces
½ pound asparagus,
  chopped into 1-inch
  pieces
¼ pound cauliflower,
  separated into florets
¼ pound carrots, peeled
  and chopped
3 tablespoons extra virgin
  olive oil
Sea salt

**SERVES FOUR**

*As any one of the three Amóstegui sisters (see page 90) of Pamplona will quickly tell you, the way to properly prepare a* menestra *is to first boil each of the component vegetables lightly and separately in unsalted fresh water so they retain their individual flavors and colors. Then gently fold them together in a little extra virgin olive oil and warm them through over a low heat. A* menestra *is a delicate dish and is certainly not, as some would have it, a stew.*

*Menestras are particularly popular in the northern regions of Rioja and Navarra, of which Pamplona is the capital, and are best come spring when broad beans, green beans, peas, and carrots are all new-season and at their sweetest. Certain recipes for* menestras *incorporate breadcrumbs, garlic, sautéed onion, pimentón, hard-boiled egg, and even saffron, but these ingredients only obscure the essence of the dish; they bulk out meager rations and disguise substandard vegetables. A little chopped cured ham added at the end is a commonplace* menestra *ingredient, but if your vegetables are of a good quality you will neither need it nor want it. Use an extra virgin olive oil of your choice (see page 13)—a* picual *will add a touch of pepper; an* arbequina, *a softer, fruitier finish. Plunge your vegetables in ice water after they have been boiled to help retain their color: a* menestra *is always better for color.*

Prepare a large bowl of ice water. Wash the chard and separate the leaves from the stems. Cut the tender parts of the stalks into 1-inch lengths and tear the leaves by hand into pieces approximately 3 inches by 3 inches. Shell the peas and broad beans.

Cook the chard stems, peas, broad beans, green beans, asparagus, cauliflower, and carrots separately in their own boiling water for approximately 5 minutes so they remain firm. Drain each and plunge into ice water, drain again, and set aside.

Gently heat the olive oil over medium-low heat in a large frying pan. Add the chard leaves, coating well with the oil. When the chard begins to wilt (after a minute or so), add the rest of the ingredients and fold to combine well. Heat through for approximately 3 minutes. Serve and sprinkle with salt to taste at the table.

# Espinacas y Garbanzos
## SPINACH AND CHICKPEAS

1/2 pound fresh spinach

1/4 cup extra virgin olive oil

1 medium yellow or white onion, chopped

2 3/4 cups cooked chickpeas

1 clove garlic, chopped

Sea salt

**SERVES FOUR**

*There's a nuttiness to chickpeas that couldn't better complement the iron edge of spinach, and the contrast in textures is just as good. The origins of this dish are Lenten, but it's now eaten year-round—you won't come across many restaurants or tapas bars in Spain that don't feature it in one guise or another. You can use an equal amount of chard instead of spinach.*

Wash the spinach well, remove any tough stalks, and if large, tear the leaves roughly by hand.

Bring 1/2 cup water to a rolling boil in a deep frying pan. Add the spinach and cook for 2 minutes, until properly wilted. Place in a sieve and remove any excess water by pressing the spinach against the sieve with the back of a spoon.

Clean the pan and gently heat the olive oil over low heat. Add the onion to the pan. Sauté over low heat for 10 minutes, or until it is soft but not brown. Add the chickpeas, stirring well to coat with the oil, and warm through for 5 minutes. Add the garlic to the onion and chickpeas. Stir well and cook for 2 minutes.

Add the spinach, mixing it well with the chickpeas and heat for 2 minutes. Add salt to taste.

**NOTE:** This is very good served alongside a seared tuna steak or grilled lamb chops or *morcilla* (blood sausage).

# Espinacas a la Catalana

## SPINACH WITH PINE NUTS AND RAISINS

*This is the Catalans' favorite way with spinach and may be an acquired taste. In the Mediterranean Balearic Islands,* Espinacas a la Catalana *is a common* empanada *(turnover) filling, the dry, short-crust pastry acting as a welcome counter to the oily sweetness. Some versions include chickpeas, which have the same effect.*

2 rounded tablespoons pine nuts
2 rounded tablespoons raisins
Boiling water
1 medium yellow or white onion, chopped
$1/4$ cup extra virgin olive oil
2 cloves garlic, chopped
1 pound spinach, well washed and roughly torn by hand
Sea salt

**SERVES FOUR**

Lightly toast the pine nuts in a dry frying pan. Put the raisins to plump up in boiling water for 10 minutes. Drain. Cook the onion slowly in the olive oil for 10 minutes, until soft but not brown. Add the garlic and cook for 2 minutes more. Add the spinach, coating it well with the oil. Stir in the pine nuts and raisins. Cook slowly, uncovered, for 10 minutes, or until the spinach has wilted. Add salt to taste.

**VARIATION:** The other commonplace Catalan way of serving spinach is creamed with a cheese crust. Follow the above instructions, but dispense with the pine nuts, raisins, and half of the olive oil. When the spinach has wilted, stir in $3/4$ cup heavy cream. Transfer to a shallow baking dish and scatter a handful of grated mild cheese over the top. Place under the broiler or in a medium oven for 5 minutes, or until the cheese is crisp and brown.

*Chard is also commonly prepared a la catalana.*

# Arroz Negro
## BLACK RICE

4¼ cups Fish Stock (page 18)

2½ tablespoons olive oil

1 small yellow or white onion, chopped

3 cloves garlic, finely chopped

2 ripe tomatoes, skinned and grated (see page 17)

1 pound cuttlefish or squid, cleaned, ink sacs reserved

1 packet or 1 teaspoon squid ink (optional)

2½ cups short-grain rice, preferably Spanish Bomba

**SERVES FOUR TO SIX**

*An arresting dish, as deeply dark and saline in appearance as it is in taste. It's made with cuttlefish, the blackness coming from its ink. You can always use squid but cuttlefish is better: it's sweeter and fleshier and its ink is thicker. Arroz Negro is firmly Catalan in origin and is best and traditionally eaten with a stiff, garlic-heavy Allioli (page 154).*

*If your fishmonger won't remove the ink sacs from the cuttlefish or squid for you, you will find them—grayish white, and one-half inch or so across— around about the starting point of the tentacles. Remove them with care. If you do not have access to fresh ink, there are packets or jars that, while obviously lacking the quality of freshness, work perfectly well.*

Heat the stock to a simmer in a saucepan. Heat the olive oil in a *paella* pan, *cazuela*, or iron frying pan (18 to 22 inches diameter is the ideal size; 14 inches is the absolute minimum). Slowly cook the onion in the olive oil until it is translucent, about 20 minutes, stirring regularly. Add the garlic. Stir well. Add the tomatoes and stir well.

Roughly chop the cuttlefish and add to the pan, stirring well. Place the ink sacs in a sieve and, using the back of a spoon, work the ink into the pan. If your squid came already cleaned, add the purchased ink now. Stir well.

Add the rice, stirring and coating it well with the ink mixture. Gently pour the hot stock into the pan through the sieve (to remove any residual ink). Stir gently and ensure the rice is spread evenly.

Cook on medium-low heat, moving the pan around slightly over the heat source every 3 to 4 minutes, for approximately 20 minutes, until the rice is of the consistency you want. Let it stand for 10 minutes off the heat before serving.

**NOTE:** You can always add other ingredients such as chunks of monkfish, shrimp, or clams to an *Arroz Negro,* but as they will all but get lost in the darkness, it is just as well to keep ingredients to a minimum.

# Sopa de Ostra Estilo Pontevedra

## OYSTER SOUP, PONTEVEDRA STYLE

*Pontevedra is the most representative of small, well-ordered, granite-built, cross-in-the-square Galician towns. It stands stolidly, some ten miles from the Atlantic coast, at the inland tip of the deep and quietly churning Ria de Pontevedra (rias being Galician fjords), a prized natural oyster bed. This might appear a heavy-handed way to treat oysters, but it is one that results in something worth overcoming inhibitions to experience.*

24 oysters
6 cups Fish Stock (page 18)
2 cups cubed bread, crusts removed
2 tablespoons olive oil
Sea salt

**SERVES FOUR**

Open the oysters, reserving their liquid. Mash the oysters to a pulp with a mortar and pestle. Heat the stock in a large pan and add the oysters and their liquid. Simmer over medium-low heat for 30 minutes. Meanwhile, gently fry the bread in the olive oil until crisp and golden. Drain on paper towels.

Strain the soup, add salt to taste, and serve topped with the croutons.

# Sopa de Ajo
## GARLIC SOUP

2¹⁄₂ heads garlic
¹⁄₄ cup olive oil
1 cup day-old white bread, cubed
1 heaping teaspoon sweet *pimentón*
4¹⁄₂ cups water or chicken stock
1 bay leaf (optional)
Sea salt
4 eggs

SERVES FOUR

*Spain's ages-old pick-me-up dates from hard times past and—in the Spanish way—is probably now coveted as much for sentimental reasons as it is for its reassuringly reviving qualities. Common to every region of Spain, sopa de ajo is also one of the country's few national dishes (tortilla de patatas, potato omelette, is probably the only other one). While the original ingredients were stale bread, wild garlic, salt, water, and oil for the more fortunate, the contemporary version normally includes egg (either poached, baked on top, or stirred in at the end), pimentón, and—and though purists desist—chicken stock in place of the water. It is a truism that Sopa de Ajo tastes better served in cazuelas (earthenware dishes, see page 10 and opposite), and if you are using them, you can always poach the eggs on top of the stove instead of baking them in the oven.*

Preheat the oven to 350°F.

Peel the cloves of 1¹⁄₂ of the heads of garlic (about 14 cloves). Gently fry them in the olive oil in a heavy frying pan that is big enough to take the water for approximately 10 minutes, or until golden but not brown. Remove and set aside.

Add the bread to the pan, stir well, and brown lightly. Add the *pimentón*. Heat the water separately and add to the pan, stirring well. Add the bay leaf, if using. Add the whole unpeeled head of garlic. Medium-chop the fried cloves of garlic and reintroduce them to the pan. Bring to a boil, then simmer for 25 minutes. Add salt to taste.

In the meantime, heat 4 single-serving size *cazuelas* or ovenproof soup bowls in the oven. Remove the head of garlic and bay leaf and spoon the soup into single portion *cazuelas* or ovenproof bowls, taking care to scoop up the garlic and breadcrumbs from the bottom of the pan. Gently break the eggs over the top of the soup. Place in the oven for 5 minutes or until the whites of the eggs are lightly set and the yolks still runny.

**VARIATION:** *Sopa castellana* (Castilian soup) is *Sopa de Ajo* with *chorizo* sausage and/or cured ham. It's from the central, upstanding regions of Castile-León and Castile-La Mancha, where, on once inquiring in a restaurant "What is *sopa castellana*?" a friend met with the simple answer, "Honest." Add four rounded tablespoons of diced *chorizo* and/or ham to the pan with the water or stock.

*Sopa de Ajo* from the parts of Andalusia and Extremadura that border Portugal can include fresh cilantro (two rounded tablespoons, medium chopped) in place of *pimentón*.

1. Soak in water overnight.

2. Fill with fresh water and cook off over a low heat.

3. Rinse before use.

# Xató

## ESCAROLE, SALT COD, TUNA, AND ANCHOVIES WITH ROMESCO DRESSING

### The romesco *dressing*

4 small dried sweet red
  peppers (see page 15)
4 tomatoes
1 tablespoon blanched
  almonds (about 12)
3/4 tablespoon hazelnuts
  (about 12)
3 cloves garlic, peeled
2 tablespoons fresh
  breadcrumbs
1 small dried red chile
1 tablespoon red wine
  vinegar
4 to 6 tablespoons extra
  virgin olive oil

### The salad

1 large head escarole
1/2 pound salt cod
  (desalted and ready to
  eat, page 16)
3/4 cup canned tuna
  (preferably in chunks)
8 anchovy fillets
16 unpitted, salted black
  olives, preferably
  *empeltre*
16 unpitted green olives,
  preferably *arbequina*

SERVES FOUR

*Rust red* romesco *dressing is very much the dominant ingredient of Xató, so don't worry too much if you do not have access to salt cod: the dish will work perfectly well if you substitute fresh cod or simply make do without. Xató is one of Spain's most distinct and delicious dishes and it comes from somewhere on or just inland from the southern Catalan coast between Barcelona and Tarragona. "Somewhere" because nine towns and villages (Calafell, Canyelles, Cubelles, Cunit, El Vendrell, Sant Pere de Ribes, Sitges, Vilafranca del Penedès, and Vilanova i la Geltrú, if you are interested) either lay claim to it or at least claim to produce the perfect example. In that it includes tomato, the recipe below represents what could be called a classic* romesco *and is more typical of Sant Pere de Ribes. Should you be interested in sampling the other versions (they tend to differ only in how the escarole is chopped or torn up and whether the dressing is spooned over or mixed in, includes tomato or not, and both almonds and hazelnuts or just the one or the other) there exists between November and April the Ruta del Xató (the Xató Tour), a moving feast of sorts in which numerous restaurants in each of the towns present their best efforts.*

For the *romesco*, boil the dried sweet peppers for 20 minutes or until they have softened. Meanwhile, preheat the oven to 250°F and roast the tomatoes for approximately 20 minutes, until they have softened and their skins loosened. Set the peppers and tomatoes aside to cool.

Toast the almonds, hazelnuts, and garlic cloves by rolling them around in a dry frying pan over a low heat for 10 minutes. Add the breadcrumbs, mix well, transfer to a mortar or food processor and reduce to a paste.

Crumble and add the dried chile. Peel and seed the tomatoes and add to the mixture. Cut the peppers in half, seed them, scrape off their flesh with a knife and add it to the mixture. Add the vinegar and 2 table-

Vilafranca del Penedès

Cangelles

Sant Pere de Ribes

Sitges

Vilanova i la Geltrú

Cubelles

El Vendrell   Cunit

Calafell

Mar Mediterráneo

spoons of olive oil. Mix well and add salt to taste. Add more oil as necessary until you have something that is the consistency of cooked oatmeal.

Tear the escarole into bite-size pieces and wash and dry it. Place half the *romesco* in a large salad bowl. Add the escarole and mix well. Add more of the *romesco* to taste. Transfer to plates, placing pieces of salt cod and tuna around the edge of each serving and the anchovies and olives on top.

**NOTE:** *Romesco* is also commonly served alongside grilled or griddled *bacalao* (salt cod). Use any white fish steaks or fillets if you do not have *bacalao* and brush them with olive oil before subjecting them to a very high temperature until they are charred and chewy at the edges.

*If you cannot find empeltre or arbequina olives, any cured black and green olives will do.*

# Remojón

## ORANGE, SALT COD, AND POTATO SALAD

2 pounds white potatoes,
  unpeeled
10 ounces desalted salt
  cod (see page 16) or
  fresh cod
2 small sweet yellow or
  white onions, peeled
4 oranges
¾ cup extra virgin olive oil
  (*picual*, if you can)
2 tablespoons sherry
  vinegar
5 ounces black olives,
  halved and pitted
Sea salt
Escarole (optional)
Pomegranate seeds
  (optional)

**SERVES FOUR**

*This recipe is from Andalusia, which is probably best visited in March and April when the* azahar *(orange blossom) is full and the air warm and perfumed like nowhere else.* Remojón *was originally a staple of the* segadores, *those who scythed down and brought in the wheat. It's both wholesome and refreshing and is best made the day before and refrigerated overnight so it can chill and the flavors can find each other while it is doing so. This version comes courtesy of Antonio Torres and Luis Oruezábal, co-owners and chef and maître d' supreme of the fine Chikito restaurant in Granada, who hand-select the oranges for their* Remojón *in the nearby valley of Lecrín, where the* azahar *is particularly impressive.*

Gently boil the potatoes. When they are done and have cooled, peel them, cut them into smallish cubes, and, importantly, leave them to dry thoroughly.

Break the cod into small pieces with your hands, removing any bones. Cut the onion into thin rings. Squeeze the juice from two of the oranges and set aside. Peel the other two oranges, removing all the pith. Segment the flesh, discard any seeds, and chop the orange flesh.

Place the orange flesh in a large bowl. Add the orange juice, the olive oil, the vinegar, and the olives. Add salt to taste and mix well. Add the onion, potatoes, and cod. Mix well and leave overnight in the fridge.

Serve, if preferred, with escarole and a few fresh scarlet pomegranate (*granada* in Spanish) seeds on top.

Luis Oruezábal, born in Buenos Aires of parents from Burgos in the north of Spain, was a professional soccer player with Granada Club de Fútbol before injury brought his career to a premature end at the age of twenty-six. A gourmet, he approached Antonio Torres, whom he thought to be the best chef in the city, and suggested they open a restaurant together. And so, in 1976, they took over Chikito. It was a good idea and—as all the photos on the walls attest—they regularly play host to certain royalty and aristocracy; bullfighters and their entourages; flamenco singers, dancers, and guitarists; cabaret and music hall artists; certain politicians; many soccer players and associated models; actors, actresses, directors, and producers of cinema and theater; painters and writers: all that is contemporary Spanish society.

# Alcachofas a la Montilla

## ARTICHOKES WITH MONTILLA-MORILES WINE

3 pounds artichokes (any size will do)

½ lemon

2 tablespoons extra virgin olive oil

1 medium yellow or white onion, chopped medium

2 cloves garlic, chopped

6 to 8 leaves fresh mint

¾ cup Montilla-Moriles wine, or dry white wine or sherry of your choice

Sea salt

Black pepper

**SERVES FOUR**

*Spain's thriving food markets are a national treasure and the best way of seeing what produce a region has to offer; the stallholders are often the most reliable sources for knowing how best to eat it and where. I arrived at Córdoba's Taberna Salinas (established 1879) by way of the city's considerable Sanchez Peña market, looking for the region's especially good artichokes poached in Montilla-Moriles, the light, white, slightly yeasty wine from the nearby towns of Montilla and Moriles (which, incidentally, is where the term* amontillado—*applied to a dry fino sherry that is given extra time in the barrel—comes from). Alas, there were no artichokes on the menu, but the restaurant's owner, Manuel Giménez, more than lived up to all that is often said about Andaluz hospitality by very kindly running home to pick up a recipe. And this—with the omission of flour and with the artichokes first being blanched instead of boiled soft—is a slightly lighter, cleaner version of it.*

*These artichokes are particularly good with roast lamb or kid.*

Bring a large pan of water to a boil. Prepare a large bowl of ice water. Clean and trim the artichokes (see page 8), wipe them all over with the lemon, and blanch them in the boiling water for 1 minute. Drain the artichokes and plunge them in the ice water so they retain their color.

Gently heat the olive oil in a *cazuela* or frying pan and add the onion. Cook over low heat for approximately 10 minutes, stirring regularly. Stir the garlic into the onion. Cook for 10 minutes more, until the onion and garlic are soft but not browned. Finely chop the mint and add to the onion.

Slice the artichokes into rounds of $^1/_2$ inch and add them and the wine to the onion mixture, raising the heat until the wine bubbles. Reduce the heat to medium and add $^1/_2$ cup water and salt and pepper to taste. Stir well. Cook over medium-low heat for 10 to 15 minutes, until most of the liquid has evaporated and the artichokes are tender.

**NOTE:** If you are using young, fresh artichokes (see page 8) there is no need to remove the chokes before cooking.

# Caldo Gallego

## GALICIAN PORK, BEANS, AND GREENS SOUP

3⁄4 pounds salt-cured shoulder, knuckle, or ribs of pork (or uncured pork slab bacon or a mixture of the two)

1¹⁄4 cups dried broad beans or large white beans

2 ounces diced salt pork or lard

3 medium potatoes, peeled

1¹⁄2 pound *grelos*, mustard greens, collards, chard, or spinach

2 small *chorizos* or pork sausages of 1 ounce each (optional)

Salt (optional)

**SERVES FOUR**

*In Galicia they leave the turnips to the cows but treat the tops with the greatest reverence. Grelos are punchily bitter greens and the essential ingredient in Galicia's triumvirate of everyday dishes which are* caldo gallego, pote gallego, *and* lacon con grelos *(as a* pote *is a more substantial* caldo *and* lacon *is cured pork shoulder, they are all actually rather similar). And certain émigré Galicians go so far as to have turnip seeds mailed to them from the homeland so they can grow their own.*

*This filling, classically basic* Caldo Gallego *is from Hector López, chef at España (established 1906), the oldest restaurant in the famously Roman-walled inland Galician town of Lugo. Mustard greens or collards work well in place of the grelos. Purists desist, but a* chorizo *or two added with the salt pork or lard can deepen the flavor. The salt pork and the beans will need to be soaked overnight.*

Soak the cured pork and the beans separately overnight.

Drain, place together in a large pot with 10 cups water, and bring to a boil. Reduce the heat to a simmer and skim off any gray foam. Add the salt pork or lard and 1 whole potato. Simmer gently for approximately 1 hour.

In the meantime, wash and coarsely chop the *grelos*. Cut the remaining potatoes into cubes of about 1¹⁄2 inches.

After the beans and pork have cooked for an hour, add the chopped *grelos*, potatoes, and *chorizos*, if using. Stir well and cook for another 35 minutes or until all the ingredients are tender.

**NOTE:** Salt curing is an ancient means of preserving meat that strongly survives in Spain. If you are using salt-cured pork, only add salt, if required, at the very end. And note that you might (depending on the cure) need to soak it before use—follow your butcher's or the package instructions.

# Alboronía

## QUINCE, SQUASH, AND EGGPLANT IN TOMATO SAUCE

*A sweet ratatouille of sorts that goes perfectly with roast pork, though that would certainly not have been the idea when it was first conceived. Alboronía comes from the Mediterranean coast of Andalusia and legend has it that its name derives from that of the princess al-Buran, wife of the ninth-century caliph al-Ma'mun, in an age when Spain took its orders from Baghdad.*

Half-fill a large saucepan with salted water and bring to a boil. Add the squash, eggplant, and quince and cook at a rolling boil for 15 minutes, until the squash and quince are barely tender.

Drain the squash, eggplant, and quince and leave to dry in a colander or large sieve. Sauté the onion and pepper in the olive oil in a *cazuela* or deep frying pan for 15 minutes, or until soft. Add the tomatoes to the onion and green pepper. Stir well and cook on low heat for 20 minutes. Add the squash, eggplant, and quince, stir well and cook for another 10 minutes. Add salt to taste.

1 pound butternut or other winter squash, peeled and cut into 1-inch chunks

1 pound eggplant, cut into 1-inch chunks

2 ripe quince, peeled, cored, and cut into 1-inch chunks

2 medium yellow or white onions, cut into strips

1 small green bell pepper

3 tablespoons extra virgin olive oil

2 pounds ripe tomatoes, peeled and chopped

Sea salt

**SERVES FOUR**

# Gazpachuelo
## SHRIMP AND MONKFISH SOUP WITH MAYONNAISE

1/2 cup extra virgin olive oil

2 eggs yolks and whites, separated and lightly beaten

Sea salt

1 lemon

1 pound white potatoes, peeled and cut into 1 1/2-inch by 1 1/2-inch chunks

1 pound monkfish, cut into 1 1/2-inch by 1 1/2-inch chunks

1/2 pound uncooked shrimp, peeled

**SERVES FOUR**

*This is a famous old fishermen's soup from the dusty, pleasantly raffish Mediterranean port city of Málaga in Andalusia. Cooked on board out at sea, the final ingredients were ultimately (and obviously) dictated by the contents of the day's catch, though the basis has always been boiled potatoes and white fish with an enriching mayonnaise folded in at the end. A highly soothing dish, this version comes from my friend Mari Poyatos's home kitchen in Algeciras—just fifteen miles across the Straits of Gibraltar from Morocco—where, as in many Spanish kitchens, it is tradition for all present to fight over the bowl in which the mayonnaise was made.*

*You can use any firm-fleshed white fish that you have on hand.*

Prepare a mayonnaise by whisking 1/2 cup of extra virgin olive oil very gradually into two beaten egg yolks until the mixture thickens. Add a pinch of salt and, if you choose, a small squeeze of lemon. Set aside.

Boil the potatoes in 6 cups of salted water until they are almost cooked. Add the monkfish and shrimp. Stir well and cook for another 5 minutes, or until the potatoes are done. Gently spoon the egg whites over the top of the soup. Cover the pan and turn off the heat. Let the mixture stand and cool, covered, for 10 minutes.

Remove the solidified egg white, chop it fine, and set aside. Slowly add a ladleful of the soup liquid to the mayonnaise, stirring as you go, and then stir the mixture back into the soup, combining it well. Sprinkle with the chopped egg white. It is traditional to mash the potatoes in the soup before eating them. Serve with lemon juice and additional salt to taste.

**NOTE:** You can make a light stock from the heads and shells of the shrimp and use it in place of the water.

**VARIATION:** Another version (and a famous one at that) of *Gazpachuelo* is *Sopa Viña AB* (Viña AB Soup, Viña AB being an amontillado sherry). To try it, add a small glass of Viña AB or any dry or medium sherry to the soup at the same time that you add the fish, or whisk it into the mayonnaise.

# Segundos Platos

## (MAIN COURSES)

Arroz a Banda ✇ Merluza en Salsa Verde ✇ Bacalao a la Llauna ✇ Chorizo a la Parapanda ✇ Cocido Madrileño ✇ Estofado de Perdiz con Macarrones ✇ Fabada ✇ Ternasco Asado ✇ Rape a la Malagueña ✇ Vicente Pérez's Cerdo con Tomate a los Vinos de la Tierra ✇ Jarrete con Castañas ✇ Mar i Muntanya ✇ Pichón Estofado ✇ Rabo de Toro ✇ Escudella Barrejada ✇ Pollo al Ajillo ✇ Sofrit Pagés ✇ Cordero en Chilindrón ✇ Fricandó ✇ Alubias Blancas con Almejas ✇ Chocos con Garbanzos ✇ Gambas con Garbanzos ✇ Solomillo de Cerdo Adobado ✇ Lomo a la Malagueña ✇ Marmitako ✇ Cordero a la Pastoril ✇ Atún Encebollado ✇ Bacalao a la Vizcaína ✇ Merluza al Albariño ✇ Caldereta de Sardinas ✇ Jarrete de Buey Estofado al Vino de Albariño ✇ Tolosanas ✇ Dorada a la Sal ✇ Caldereta de Llagosta ✇

# Arroz a Banda
## RICE WITH POACHED FISH

4 pounds mixed whole fish
  (bream, monkfish tail,
  bass, mullet, or
  scorpionfish, but nothing
  oily)
16 mussels
1 medium yellow or white
  onion
1 bay leaf
4 cloves garlic, peeled
2 ñoras (small dried red
  peppers) or ½ teaspoon
  of *pimentón*
4 medium tomatoes
½ cup white wine
  (optional)
Sea salt
3 tablespoons olive oil
8 large shrimp, unpeeled
8 clams
*Allioli* (page 154)
6 threads saffron
2 cups short-grain rice
  preferably Spanish
  Bomba

**SERVES FOUR**

Arroz a Banda *(literally, "rice on the side") can appear gray and uninspiring—the antithesis of the flashiest saffron and shrimp-pink paella—but it is one of Spain's greatest and most popular rice dishes. Fish are filleted, poached in a stock made from their heads and bones and any available crustacea, and eaten with garlic mashed with olive oil (see* Allioli, *page 154). Rice is then cooked paella-style in the fish broth and eaten as a separate course.*

Arroz a banda *comes from the rice fields of Alicante, the southernmost province of Valencia, and, as is generally the way with Spanish fish-based rices and stews, is something of a lucky dip with regard to the fish that goes into it. The clever, slightly spicy, and cheering method of adding the* salsa salmorra *to the rice in the cooking here (it is more usually served on the side, which is what you should do if you want a traditional* arroz a banda*) is the way that Mari Carmen Vélez and Norberto Vera do it at the busy La Sirena (The Mermaid) just outside Alicante town, where, every lunchtime Tuesday through Sunday, three out of every four customers order whichever of their grand repertoire of* arrozes *they are preparing that day.*

Fillet the fish and place their heads and bones, half of the mussels, half the onion, the bay leaf, 1 whole clove of garlic, the dried red peppers (whole) and 1 tomato, cut in two, in a large pan. Add 6 cups water and the wine, if using, and bring to the boil. Reduce the heat and simmer for 15 minutes before removing the dried peppers and setting them aside to cool. Continue to simmer the stock for 30 minutes more.

Meanwhile, start to prepare the *salsa salmorra* by mashing the remaining 3 cloves of garlic together in a mortar with a pinch of salt and 1 tablespoon of the olive oil. Add the remaining 3 tomatoes, skinned and seeded (see page 17). Cut or tear open the peppers, carefully remove their seeds with your fingers or by rinsing under cold running water, and scrape off their flesh with a sharp knife. Add the pepper flesh to the garlic and tomatoes in the mortar to finish the *salsa salmorra.*

Strain the stock into another large pan and continue to simmer.

Heat the remaining olive oil over low heat in a paella pan or frying pan of approximately 18-inch diameter (or a minimum of 14 inches). Medium-chop the remaining onion half and cook for approximately 15 minutes, until it is soft but not browned.

Meanwhile, bring the stock to a gentle boil and poach the fillets of fish, shrimp, clams, and the remaining mussels for 5 to 10 minutes, or until they are done. Remove the fish, shrimp, clams, and mussels from the stock with a slotted spoon and serve with *Allioli* while the rice is cooking.

Add the *salsa salmorra* to the onion, stir well, and reduce for 2 minutes. Add the saffron and 3$^1$⁄$_2$ cups of hot stock. Add the rice, spread it evenly and cook over a low to medium-low heat, moving the pan slightly every 5 minutes to spread the heat, for approximately 20 minutes, until it has all but absorbed the stock.

# Merluza en Salsa Verde

## HAKE IN GREEN SAUCE WITH CLAMS

One 2 to 2½-pound hake, or scrod or any white fish

3 tablespoons olive oil

½ small yellow or white onion, finely chopped

2 cloves garlic, finely chopped

¼ cup dry white wine (at Castelló 9 they use a good-to-middling Verdejo from Castile-León)

24 little neck clams or cockles

1 tablespoon chopped flat-leaf parsley

Sea salt

**SERVES FOUR**

*There's a trick that elevates this dish—Spain's favorite way with what is its favorite fish—to something very special, and I am indebted to José Martínez and Miguel Ángel Rodriguez, front of house and chef, respectively, of the fine fish restaurant Castelló 9 in Madrid, for letting me in on it. The thing to do—or, at least, the thing they do—is to make the stock from the fish's own bones, head, and (here's the trick) skin. The result, with the addition of white wine, clams, and half a handful of parsley, is a deliciously deep, viscous sauce that should transport you at least some way to the very sea from which your fish came.*

Fillet the fish (or have your fishmonger do it for you). Place the head, bones, and skin in 3 cups water and cook over medium heat for approximately 30 minutes, until the water has reduced to 2 cups or so. Skim off any gray foam that forms on top of the stock. Strain the stock and set aside.

Heat the olive oil over medium heat in a large frying pan. Add the onion and garlic to the oil, stirring well. Immediately add the fish, cooking it for approximately 30 seconds on each side.

Pour over the wine and the stock so they just cover the fish (quickly turn the fish once if the liquid doesn't quite cover it). With the heat still on medium, cook until the sauce begins to bubble, then remove the fish and keep it warm. Stir the sauce well and add the clams. When the clams open, remove them from the sauce, stir in the parsley and add salt to taste. Pour the sauce over the fish and serve surrounded with the clams.

*There's an immediate feeling of being closer to the sky in Madrid. Spain's capital sits high up on the central plain right in the middle of the country, and draws its influences—and, not least, what it eats—from all points around. And, as capital cities tend to, Madrid enjoys a fine reputation— fairly accorded, to the most part—for eating well, particularly with regard to fish, which has long been express-delivered to the city directly from the boat. Arrivals that Madrileños particularly look out for (and sincere thanks to the fishmonger brothers Alonso at the city's La Latina market, as jolly personally as they are serious about what they sell, for educating me in this) include the first* salmonetes *(red mullet) from the small town of Santa Pola in Alicante in January; Mediterranean horse mackerel and* boquerones *(an anchovy of sorts) from Málaga in February; bonito tuna from Cantabria and red tuna from the southern* almadraba *(see page 113) in June and July; and the very best* percebes *(gooseneck barnacles), spider crabs, and clams from Galicia in December. Most fish in Madrid is eaten* natural, *which means plain grilled, baked, or cooked on a plancha (flat griddle), and any recipes used invariably come from where the fish was landed. Indeed,* Merluza en Salsa Verde *is also known as* merluza a la vasca *(hake in the Basque way).*

# Bacalao a la Llauna

## BAKED SALT COD WITH TOMATO, ONION, PIMENTÓN, AND WHITE WINE

1½ pounds salt cod, desalted (page 16) and cut in pieces, or 4 white fish fillets or tuna steaks

All-purpose flour

2 tablespoons olive oil

1 medium yellow or white onion, finely chopped

1 bay leaf

2 cloves garlic, finely chopped

6 ripe tomatoes, skinned and seeded (see page 17)

1 heaped teaspoon sweet *pimentón* or paprika

½ cup dry white wine

**SERVES FOUR**

*This is Catalonia's most celebrated contribution to Spain's million and one ways with* bacalao *(salt cod) and quite possibly the most popular* Menú *dish in that region's capital, Barcelona. Certainly, it's a favorite at Bar Blanca, a café (in the best, revolving-community-unto-itself sense of the word) presided over by a jolly young Alan Alda look-alike, and situated opposite the fresh herb and exotica stall in the city's excellent Sant Antoni market.*

*If you don't have* bacalao *at hand, don't worry: this dish works equally well with any white fish or even tuna steaks. It's also good for a dinner party as you can do everything but the baking in advance. Serve with a few lima beans, chickpeas, or plain boiled potatoes livened up with a good olive oil and a handful of chopped parsley or chives. Llauna, incidentally, is Catalan for "tin."*

Preheat the oven to 400°F.

Dust the fish with flour and sauté in the olive oil in a large frying pan over medium heat for 5 minutes, turning once.

Remove the fish from the pan, set aside, and add the onion. Cook over low heat for 15 minutes, until soft but not browned. Add the bay leaf. Add the garlic to the onion. Add the tomatoes and stir well. Raise the heat to medium. Add the *pimentón* and wine. Stir well and leave for 10 minutes to reduce.

Warm a lightly oiled baking dish in the oven. Place the fish on the dish and cover each piece with a good tablespoonful or two of the tomato and onion mixture. Bake for 10 minutes and serve.

*As popular as* Bacalao a la Llauna *is, Catalonia's national dish (and another* Menú del Día *mainstay) is undoubtedly* butifarra amb mongetes. Butifarra *is a pork sausage that doubles as an unofficial national symbol of Catalonia, and* mongetes *are small white beans, the best ones coming from the volcanic soil of Ganxet in the Pyrenees, something, say the Catalans, that accounts for their not causing flatulence. The butifarra is either grilled or fried and the mongetes are lightly fried in olive oil and perhaps a little garlic so they crisp on the outside while remaining soft and creamy in the middle. Numerous—too numerous to mention here—cured butifarras are also produced.*

# Chorizo a la Parapanda

## FRESH CHORIZO WITH FRIED EGGS

*Antonio López produces exceptionally good organic olive oil in the highlands of the Sierra de Parapanda, some twenty miles west of Granada in Andalusia. His production is a little unusual in that—the expected* picual *aside—it includes a 100 percent* lucio, *a puckishly bitter and spicy oil, more yellow than green in color and much more normally blended than left on its own. And certainly no other oil works as well as a lucio in cutting through the slippery richness of* Chorizo a la Parapanda, *which is the attractively messy way the shepherds of the Sierra de Parapanda have always prepared fresh* chorizo *and fried eggs. This is a natural brunch or supper dish and is best eaten with good bread and in relaxed company. Use a coarse pork or Italian sausage if you do not have access to fresh* chorizo.

8 fresh *chorizos* or pork sausages, about 2 pounds
8 fresh eggs
¼ cup extra virgin olive oil (preferably *lucio*), plus additional for serving
Red or white wine vinegar
Sea salt

**SERVES FOUR**

---

Fry the *chorizos* and eggs in separate pans in 2 tablespoons olive oil each. Once they are done, place on a paper towel to remove as much of the oil as possible. Place the *chorizos* and eggs on a large serving plate and roughly chop them up with a knife and fork. Mix well, adding fresh oil, vinegar, and salt to taste.

**NOTE:** For Antonio's oil, see Resources (page 159).

# Cocido Madrileño

## MADRID-STYLE MIXED MEAT AND CHICKPEA STEW

8 heaping tablespoons
dried chickpeas (Celia's
actual measurement is 1
handful per person plus
2 for the pot)

1 pound beef shank (either
whole or in two pieces)

2 beef soup bones

2 ham bones

¼ pound *tocino* or fatty
bacon, in 1 piece

1 whole bone-in chicken
breast

1 chicken thigh

1 *chorizo* (*casero* is best;
see note, page 45)

1 large stalk celery

1 large leek, trimmed and
well washed

1 large carrot, peeled

1 large white potato,
peeled

Sea salt

1 *morcilla* (blood sausage,
optional)

1 heaping tablespoon
"*Fideos* No. 1" or fine
noodles or vermicelli

**SERVES SIX**

Insofar as every region has one, it is the cocido *rather than the very well-travelled but faithfully Valencian paella that is Spain's national dish. Cocido is a substantial, slow-cooked, one-pot stew that has its roots firmly in the Sephardic Jewish* adafina, *the meal that was prepared the day before and then simmered, untouched, on the Sabbath. Cocido is the past perfect tense of the Spanish verb* cocer, *to cook, and so simply means "cooked." Following the Reconquista (when the Christian kings wrested control of Spain from the Muslim Moors), with the addition of pork, it was adopted by all. In Valencia and the south it's known as* puchero *and in Catalonia as* Escudella *(page 94), but it is the* Cocido Madrileño *that is considered the classic of the genre.*

*In Madrid, the famous Lhardy aside, Taberna de Buenaventura and La Taberna de la Daniela produce excellent* cocidos. *But that said, it has always been more of an at-home dish, and, for that reason—as well as because it works very well—the recipe below comes, by way of their late grandmother, from brother and sister José Luis and Celia Díez, great friends and good Madrileños. The custom is to eat the broth first (with a few noodles cooked in it) and then the meat, chickpeas, and vegetables. Serve green cabbage on the side (see Note on opposite page).*

*You will need to soak the chickpeas overnight before cooking.*

⟿

Soak the chickpeas overnight in water to cover.

Fill a stockpot (8-quart capacity or more) with 5½ quarts of water and place over medium-high flame. Add the beef, bones, *tocino*, chicken, and *chorizo*. When the water comes to the boil, reduce the heat to medium-low, skim off any gray foam that has formed on top (and continue to do so at regular intervals), and add the vegetables and a good pinch of salt. Simmer for 1½ hours.

Remove from the heat, leave to cool briefly, and skim off the fat from the top.

Return to the heat, add the chickpeas, and simmer for 1 hour more, adding the *morcilla* after 40 minutes. Remove and discard the bones.

Without turning off the heat, remove the meats, vegetables, and chickpeas from the broth with a slotted spoon. Cut the meats and vegetables into serving pieces and arrange everything on a large serving dish. Keep warm. Quickly cook the noodles in the broth and serve as a first course.

**NOTE:** *Cocido* is traditionally served with a side dish of green cabbage: chop a medium head of green cabbage and boil in salted water until tender. Drain. Heat 4 tablespoons olive oil in a large frying pan over medium-low heat. Peel and thinly slice 2 cloves garlic and add to the oil. Cook for 30 seconds and add the cabbage and 1 teaspoon of sweet *pimentón*. Stir well and turn off the heat. Add 1 teaspoon white wine or sherry vinegar, stir again, cover, and leave to stand for 5 minutes before serving.

**VARIATIONS:** Celia's Murcian in-laws' *cocido* includes lamb bones, flat green beans, and a few threads of saffron.

Some people also add one or more *pelotas* (balls) made typically from chopped beef and/or pork, breadcrumbs, chopped parsley, and garlic, and beaten egg, to their *cocidos*.

Cocido *leftovers tend to appear the next day as* ropa vieja *(old clothes). Fry a sliced large white onion in a couple of tablespoons of olive oil until soft. Add any leftover chickpeas. Add any leftover meat, chopped into bite-size pieces. Stir well. Heat through thoroughly and serve.*

# Estofado de Perdiz con Macarrones

## PARTRIDGE WITH MACARONI

2 red-legged partridges, about 1 pound each (or 4 if you feel 2 are not sufficient)

3 tablespoons olive oil

1 carrot, finely chopped

1 medium white onion, chopped medium

1 small green bell pepper, chopped

1 small red bell pepper, chopped medium

3 tomatoes, seeded and chopped

4 cloves garlic, finely chopped

1 bay leaf

1 bundle of mixed herbs or 1 heaping tablespoon chopped herbs (thyme, oregano, marjoram, rosemary, parsley)

1 teaspoon grated lemon zest

1 cup dry white wine

3/4 pound macaroni, such as elbow or small shells

Sea salt

**SERVES FOUR**

*Castile—La Mancha is famous for its red-legged partridge, but neighboring Andalusia has its fair share too. The Duke of Wellington enjoys some of the best shooting on his expansive estate near Granada, an ages-old gift to his family from Spain for help in restraining the French during the Peninsular War of 1807 to 1814. The birds are eaten young and, as here, more often see the inside of a stewpot than an oven. This recipe (or at least the ingredients and method) was given to me in Cádiz, on the Atlantic Andalusian coast not too far from Portugal, the only place I had previously come across noodles stewed with game birds or fowl.*

*This dish works equally well with quail, guinea fowl, chicken, or rabbit.*

Split the partridges (or have your butcher do it for you) and brown them in the olive oil over a medium heat in a large lidded casserole. Remove and set aside.

Add the carrot, onion, and peppers to the casserole. Reduce the heat to low, and cook, stirring every 5 minutes, for approximately 25 minutes, until the vegetables are soft but not brown.

Add the tomatoes and garlic. Add the bay leaf, herbs, and lemon zest. Stir well. Add the wine and raise the heat to medium-high until it bubbles. Add 1/2 cup water and stir well. Return the partridges to the casserole, turning them in the vegetable and wine mixture. Reduce the heat and simmer, covered, for 1 hour, turning the partridges every 20 minutes and ensuring nothing is sticking to the bottom of the casserole. Remove the lid and test the partridges for doneness. If necessary, add more water and continue to cook, uncovered.

When the partridges are nearly ready (between 1 and 1 1/2 hours), add the macaroni. Raise the heat until the liquid is bubbling gently, add more water if necessary, and stir well. Remove the partridges and set aside to keep warm.

Cook the macaroni until it is the texture you prefer (the Spanish tend to cook pasta until it is approaching mushy) and add salt to taste. The end result should resemble a very thick soup.

Remove the herb bundle and bay leaf and serve the partridges and macaorni together in deep bowls.

# Fabada

## ASTURIAN WHITE BEANS WITH PORK

2¹⁄₂ cups uncooked *fabes*
 or other large, dried
 white beans
¹⁄₂ medium yellow or white
 onion, peeled
¹⁄₄ pound chorizo
 preferably smoked
¹⁄₂ pound cured ham hock
¹⁄₄-pound *tocino* or fatty
 bacon, in one piece
1 pig's ear or tail (optional)
4 threads saffron
¹⁄₄ pound *morcilla* (blood
 sausage, optional)
Sea salt

**SERVES FOUR**

*Be sure to use the smoothest, fattest white beans you can find for this. Fabada should be creamy and a touch sticky—like a French cassoulet— and powdery, unforgiving beans or those that crumble in the cooking are the bane of it. This is northwesterly Asturias's most celebrated dish and there they use their own especially good fabes (hence the name fabada, which you could translate to "fabes feast") that are more than worth making an effort to find (see Resources, page 159); butter or lima beans or any large white bean will do if you can't. You will also need an ample selection of pork and pork products (what they call compango for this purpose in Asturias) such as smoked ham, chorizo, an ear or tail, bacon, and blood sausage if possible, to give it an all-round fullness, both in body and flavor.*

*If in Asturias or thereabouts, it is worth taking a detour to try the fabada in the restaurant-cum-bar-cum-hostal-cum-post-office-cum-general-store in the village of Puerta de Cabrales, a place that is actually more famous for its cabrales, a forceful blue cheese, the more mature examples of which are capable of inducing minor facial muscle spasms. Otherwise, that at La Copita Asturiana in Madrid must be as good as any—because fabada is Spain's favorite bean dish, and because Asturians have long migrated in search of work, you will find excellent versions throughout Spain, particularly in the larger cities.*

*Don't forget that you will need to soak the beans overnight beforehand; precooked bottled and canned beans are very good things, but not here.*

~

Soak the beans overnight in cold water to cover.

Drain, rinse, and put them in a large casserole. Add the onion, and cover with cold water to a depth of 2 inches. Bring to the boil, skim off any foam that forms on the top and reduce to a simmer. Add the *chorizo*, ham hock, *tocino*, and ear, if using, taking great care not to break any of the beans. Cover and cook over very low heat for 1 hour, ensuring that the beans are always just covered with cooking liquid (add more cold water if necessary).

Toast the saffron in a dry frying pan, crush it and gently stir it into the beans. Add the *morcilla*, if using. Cover and cook for 1 hour more, until the beans are perfectly soft. Add salt to taste.

If necessary, thicken by breaking 5 or 6 beans open and quickly bringing the dish to the boil. Leave to stand off the heat for 20 minutes. Serve the beans and meats separately.

# Ternasco Asado

## ROAST SHOULDER OF LAMB WITH POTATOES

2¹⁄₂ pounds large white
   potatoes, peeled
5 to 7 tablespoons olive oil
2 to 3 cloves garlic, slivered
Sea salt
¹⁄₂ cup dry white wine
   (optional)
1 bone-in shoulder of
   lamb, approximately 3¹⁄₂
   pounds, or two smaller
   shoulders
2 tablespoons chopped
   fresh thyme or rosemary,
   or 2 rounded teaspoons
   dried
4 heads garlic, unpeeled

**SERVES FOUR**

*Asadores—the word represents both big, brick-built wood-fired ovens and the generally vast, utilitarian, often roadside restaurants that house them— are where the roasting takes place in Spain. In central Castile-León—real* asador *country—the specialty (along with suckling pig) is* lechazo, *a whole roast baby lamb of just two or three weeks of age. The other region that rightly has a reputation for its lamb is Aragón, inland from Catalonia and reaching from the Pyrenees down to Valencia. Here the lamb is eaten a little older, at a couple of months, and is known as* ternasco.

*This is a very simple, traditional Aragonese dish. It's another in the great Spanish tradition of simple one-pot affairs that, as here with the potatoes playing foil to the lamb, couldn't work better at imparting flavor.*

Bring a large pot of salted water to a boil. Cut the potatoes into slices ¹⁄₄-inch or so. Blanch them for 2 minutes. Drain and leave to cool. Meanwhile, preheat the oven to 325°F.

Put 3 tablespoons of olive oil in a large roasting pan or *cazuela* and put to heat in the oven for 5 minutes. Remove the pan from the oven and layer with the potato slices, dribbling with a little more oil and, if you like, placing a few slivers of garlic and a suggestion of salt between each level. Pour over the white wine, if using. Dribble a little more oil on top. Sprinkle a pinch of salt. Place in the oven.

Rub a couple of tablespoonfuls of olive oil vigorously into the lamb, sprinkle with a little salt and half of the herbs. Place the lamb on top of the potatoes and roast, allowing approximately 22 minutes per pound if you like your lamb pink and 28 minutes if you prefer it reasonably well done.

Dunk the heads of garlic in water and put them on top of the potatoes when 30 minutes cooking time remains.

Sprinkle with the rest of the herbs and leave to stand for 10 minutes before carving and serving. Break up the roasted garlic heads to serve with the lamb and potatoes.

**VARIATIONS:** Lamb isn't generally served pink in Spain. Rather, it's cooked long and slow until the meat can be pulled from the bone. If that is the way you like it, lower the heat to 250°F and give it forty-five minutes to an hour longer. Add the bulbs of garlic to soften and sweeten—and eventually dab on each mouthful—when you have approximately thirty minutes cooking time remaining.

Shoulders of lamb are particularly popular in Spain and are well suited to slow cooking; change the cooking time if you are using a leg or rack: approximately 20 minutes per pound for a medium-rare leg and 25 minutes per pound for a similarly cooked rack. Time it right and you will know it's done when the top of the potatoes brown and crisp.

**NOTE:** Asadores commonly serve their roasts accompanied by a romaine or escarole lettuce, dressed in oil and a sometimes overly generous amount of vinegar.

*This method of cooking also works extremely well with whole fish: try bass or bream.*

The asadores *of the Basque Country don't use ovens, but expansive, charcoal-burning ranges called* brasas. *They specialize in* chuletas—*extremely weighty "beef chops" (T-bones) of between two and a half and six pounds—and the person whose job it is to prepare them is the* brasero, *or, in Jayne Hardcastle's case, the* brasera. *English by birth (her family left Blackpool for Ibiza when she was four), Jayne is an acknowledged master* brasera *who, with her Basque husband and their sons, owns and runs three* asadores *including La Ripa in Bilbao and the famous Asador Horma Hondo in the nearby village of Bernagoitia. The Basque Country is one of the very few regions of Spain (Galicia is probably the only other one) that properly appreciates beef and, as such,* chuletas *are a serious business.*

*Traditionally,* chuletas *came from big, generously fed castrated oxen that, at the end of their working days, were permitted a few weeks to wander free, gorge themselves, and relax before being eaten. Remarkably, Jayne still manages to take delivery of these animals six times a year, though her everyday* chuletas *come from the* rubia *(blond) breed of animal of one producer in the village of Montellos in Galicia. These animals are slaughtered at between four and seven years of age, and the whole ribs are hung in the restaurant for twenty-seven to forty days to mature.*

*A* chuleta *should be at room temperature when it goes on the* brasa *and cooked approximately one inch from the charcoal, which should be nothing less than white hot. Once it is put to cook it is lightly salted on top to draw the juice of the meat away from the heat source and up toward the surface: a properly prepared* chuleta *will retain all of its juices, not spilling a drop, not even when being cut on the plate. When the* chuleta *is done on one side (after about three minutes) it is turned, the other side salted, and the process repeated. The more mature the* chuleta, *the more salt it will take. Another three minutes or so (instinct as much as practice makes a good* brasero) *and it's done. The* chuleta *should now consist of three textures: slightly crisp on the surface, rare underneath, and all but raw in the center; all good* braseros *will tell you how important it is that the heat reaches the center of the* chuleta *but only so far as to kiss it.*

# Rape a la Malagueña

## MONKFISH, MÁLAGA STYLE

*The classic Mediterranean combination of saffron and almonds makes this a special, subtle dish. The version here comes from the brothers Manuel and José Calvo, the owners of Málaga's Méson Astorga, where one day in February 2007, this dish was second of one of the most memorable three courses that anyone could ever have sat down to. (Battered eggplant with sugar cane syrup and* poleá, *an aniseed and cinnamon custard with olive-oil-fried croutons that you will find on page 137, were the first and third.) To best prepare it you will need a food processor, though a mortar and pestle will suffice.*

1½ tablespoons blanched almonds (about 18)
2 cloves garlic, peeled
6 threads saffron
1 tablespoon breadcrumbs
1 small yellow or white onion, chopped
1 small green bell pepper, chopped
1 bay leaf
¼ cup olive oil
¾ cup dry white wine
1 tablespoon chopped parsley
¾ cup Fish Stock (page 18)
Sea salt
White pepper
2½ pounds monkfish medallions, cut across the bone
All-purpose flour

**SERVES FOUR**

Prepare a *picada* (see page 89) by lightly toasting the almonds and garlic over a low heat in a large, dry frying pan or *cazuela* for 5 minutes, or until they begin to take color. Add the saffron and breadcrumbs, stir well, and crush together with a mortar and pestle or in a food processor. Set aside.

Cook the onion, green pepper, and bay leaf very slowly in 2 tablespoons of the olive oil in the pan in which you toasted the almonds, stirring regularly, for 20 minutes, or until they are soft. Add the wine and stir well. Add the *picada* and parsley, stir well, and cook for 5 minutes. Remove the bay leaf and puree the mixture in a food processor or mortar.

Heat the fish stock. Gradually add the fish stock to the *picada*, mixing until you have a sauce the consistency of a thick soup. Add salt and pepper to taste.

Clean the pan and put it over medium heat with the 2 remaining tablespoons of olive oil. Lightly dust the monkfish with flour. Quickly brown it in the oil. Remove from the pan and set aside.

Wipe the pan clean, place it over low heat, and return the monkfish to it. Pour the sauce over and heat through for 5 minutes before serving.

# Vicente Pérez's Cerdo con Tomate a los Vinos de la Tierra

## VICENTE PÉREZ'S PORK WITH TOMATO AND THE WINES OF THE COUNTRY

2 tablespoons olive oil

2¹⁄₂ pounds mixed loin, belly, and ribs of pork

1 medium yellow or white onion, finely chopped

1 medium green bell pepper, finely chopped

One 14-ounce can chopped tomatoes

³⁄₄ cup dry or medium-dry white wine (Vicente uses something slightly fruity from nearby Villanueva del Ariscal)

2 tablespoons Pedro Ximénez, sweet sherry, or dessert wine

1 tablespoon cornstarch

Sea salt

Black pepper

**SERVES FOUR TO SIX**

*Vicente Pérez worked as a traveling representative for a pharmaceutical company—enjoying most the opportunity that the position gave him to eat his way around Spain—until the advent of the year 2000 moved him to give it up and devote himself to his twin passions of food and flamenco. (Millennium Syndrome, perhaps.) And so he took over the Muralla Antigua taberna in his hometown of Seville, where he now cooks by day and sings fandango behind the bar by night. Opposite the bar there stands a large glass case that contains a stone bust of the legendary torero (bullfighter) Curro Romero and a portrait of "El Camarón" (The Shrimp), the James Dean of flamenco. This is Vicente's shrine to racial, the flamenco term that means the ability to move freely from one classic style or discipline to another; to not fear change but to embrace it and master it.*

*This is an uncomplicated dish, but it does require some slow cooking. Vicente uses the loin of the Iberian pig, but with the meat of a normal domestic pig, it works better with belly and ribs. The end result should ideally be the consistency of a hash. Vicente recommends it for brunch or supper with fried potatoes.*

Heat the olive oil in large deep pan, casserole, or heavy Dutch oven and brown the pork over medium-low heat. Remove the pork and set aside.

In the same pan, cook the onion and pepper over very low heat for approximately 15 minutes, until soft but not brown. Add the pork and combine well. Add the tomatoes and stir well. Add the wines and raise the heat until the mixture bubbles. Stir in the cornstarch. Add salt and pepper to taste. Cover and cook over a low heat, stirring occasionally, for approximately 1¹⁄₂ hours, until the pork is tender to the point of falling apart.

**NOTE:** Pedro Ximénez is the grandest grape of Andalusia. It produces a syrupy, mahogany brown, raisin-sweet wine that is drunk as an aperitif as much as it is with desserts and, as above, is also used to give sweetness to savory dishes.

Come in gentlemen, don't leave without trying a very cold, special beer!
La Muralla Antigua, March 2007

# Jarrete con Castañas

BEEF SHANK WITH CHESTNUTS

3 tablespoons lard or olive oil

3 pounds beef shank, cut across the bone into 1-inch rounds

1 large yellow or white onion, chopped

2 cloves garlic, chopped

1½ cups dry or medium-dry white wine

3 cups beef stock or water

2 sprigs fresh thyme

1 bay leaf

Sea salt

½ pound fresh chestnuts or 1 scant cup jarred chestnuts

**SERVES FOUR**

*An easy braise from the north. You know that summer has finally given way to fall in Spain when the roasted chestnut sellers appear on the street corners.*

～

Heat the lard in a large, heavy lidded pot over medium heat. Brown the beef on both sides. Remove the beef and set aside.

Lower the heat and add the onion, stirring well to coat it in the lard. Cook over low heat for approximately 15 minutes, until it is soft but not brown. Add the garlic. Stir well and cook for 5 minutes. Add the wine and bring to bubbling. Add the stock. Add the thyme, bay leaf, and a pinch of salt. Add back the beef, reduce the heat to low, cover the pan, and simmer for 2 hours, turning the beef every 30 minutes.

In the meantime, prepare the chestnuts if you're using fresh: remove a thin strip of the shell with a sharp knife and place the chestnuts in a pan of cold water. Bring the water to the boil and boil the chestnuts for 1 minute. Remove the chestnuts one by one, and peel off both the shell and bitter inner skin.

Scrape up any bits that have stuck to the bottom of the pan and add the chestnuts. Cook for another hour, adding more stock or water if necessary, until the beef is coming away from the bone and the chestnuts are soft.

# Mar i Muntanya
## CHICKEN WITH SHRIMP

½ tablespoon blanched almonds (about 6)

½ tablespoon shelled hazelnuts, or blanched, if you prefer (about 6)

6 to 8 strands saffron

1 tablespoon breadcrumbs

½ ounce grated bittersweet chocolate (70% cocoa or more)

6 tablespoons extra virgin olive oil

1 medium yellow or white onion, chopped

One 2- to 3-pound chicken cut into 8 pieces

All-purpose flour

1½ pounds large shrimp, or langoustine in the shell, or lobster, split in half lengthwise (see page 123)

3 cloves garlic, finely chopped

3 tomatoes, skinned and seeded (see page 17)

½ cup dry white wine

2 tablespoons brandy

3 cups chicken stock or water

**SERVES FOUR**

*Though my first* Mar i Muntanya *("Sea and Mountain" in Catalan) comprised surprising soft braised calves cheeks and the tiniest, gummiest baby squid, the dish is much more usually a rich hazelnut-, bread-, and chocolate-thickened marriage of chicken and shrimp or lobster. It hails from Empordà, up toward the Catalan-French border, and not so far north of the town of Palamos—home, they say, of some of the best shrimp in Spain, perhaps the world. This is an old dish, so old that it dates from the far-off age when shrimp and lobster where so plentiful they were commonly used to bolster stews of the more prized chicken. Nowadays, of course, it's the shrimp and lobster that are the luxury and, as such, the idea of subjecting them to the rigor of a* Mar i Muntanya *might not come naturally to you. But do try, because this is a true Catalan classic.*

*This recipe is based on the* Mar i Muntanya *served at the restaurant Hispania in Arenys de Mar, just south of Empordà. It was opened in 1952 in the former Hispania car garage by a family of fishmongers, the Rexachs, and specializes in traditional Catalan cuisine. Now presided over by the sisters Lolita and Paquita Rexach, it won its first Michelin star in 2005 and has more than once been cited as the best traditional restaurant in Spain.*

Lightly toast the almonds and hazelnuts in a large, dry frying pan or *cazuela*. Stir in the saffron and breadcrumbs, then crush all together in a mortar or food processor with the grated chocolate to make a *picada*. (See note on opposite page.)

Wipe the pan clean and gently heat 2 tablespoons of the olive oil over low heat. Cook the onion very slowly for 20 minutes, or until soft.

Meanwhile, dust the chicken pieces with flour and sauté over medium-low heat in another pan in the rest of the olive oil, until lightly browned. Add the shrimp to the chicken and cook, turning once, for 2 minutes. Set the chicken and shrimp aside.

Add the garlic and tomatoes to the onion. Stir well. Add the wine and brandy. Stir well and leave to bubble for 10 minutes. Warm the stock and add to the onion and tomato mixture. Stir well and simmer for 10 minutes. Strain through a fine sieve and set aside.

Rinse the pan or *cazuela*, place over low heat and put in the chicken and shrimp. Pour on the strained sauce. Add the *picada*, stir well and simmer for 5 minutes to warm through before serving.

**NOTE:** *Picadas* are used all the way along the Mediterranean coast from Andalusia to Catalonia to thicken and flavor any number of dishes. They can include garlic, fried bread, almonds, hazelnuts, pine nuts, salt, dried peppers, tomato, olive oil, any herb, saffron, cinnamon, and sometimes chocolate.

# Pichón Estofado

## STEWED PIGEON

6 tablespoons olive oil

2 large or 4 small pigeons, wild, wood pigeons or milk-fed squab

2 medium yellow or white onions, roughly chopped

1 large carrot, roughly chopped

6 cloves garlic (or more or less, if you prefer), unpeeled

1 cinnamon stick

1 quart chicken or game stock

One 750 ml bottle red wine (ideally a Navarran Tempranillo, though Rioja is fine)

Sea salt

Two 1- to 1¹⁄₂-inch thick slices of crusty bread per person

**SERVES FOUR**

*An appropriately robust way to treat pigeon from Navarra, which borders France and is almost as well known for its game as it is for its superior vegetables (see* Menestra Riojana, *page 48). This recipe comes courtesy of the Amóstegui restaurant in the city of Pamplona, domain of the three sisters Amóstegui: Marisol, Blanca, and Marina. It was once firm tradition in Spain for family restaurants to be run by the women of the house, freeing the men to take on the more physical outside work including the obvious hunting and gathering. Though this custom has now all but ended, it continues to survive strongly—and curiously—in Pamplona, a relatively small town where one can still enjoy the particular dynamic of eating in a restaurant run by sisters in four of the very best places in town: Hartza, Europa, Castillo de Gorraiz, and Amóstegui.*

*A dish of sautéed mushrooms and potatoes goes well with this.*

Quickly brown the pigeons in 3 tablespoons of the olive oil in a very deep, heavy lidded frying pan. Set the pigeons aside.

Cook the onion, carrot, and garlic in the oil in which you browned the pigeons over low heat for 10 minutes, or until soft. Add the cinnamon. Heat the stock in a separate pan. Add the wine to the onion and carrot and raise the heat until it bubbles. Add the hot stock. Add the pigeons, cover the pan and simmer for approximately 1 hour, until tender. Remove the pigeons. Press the contents of the pan through a sieve until smooth, discarding the cinnamon stick and any garlic skin. Place the sauce back in the pan, add salt to taste, and if necessary, quickly reduce over high heat until it is the consistency of a medium-thick soup. Fry two rounds of bread per person in the remaining 3 tablespoons olive oil. Split the pigeons in half, spoon over the sauce and serve with the fried bread.

**NOTE:** The liver is generally left in the pigeon during the cooking and spread on the fried bread at the table. If you do not have pigeon, substitute a stronger-tasting game bird or two quail per person.

# Rabo de Toro

## BRAISED OXTAIL

¼ cup olive oil

4 pounds fighting bulls'
tails or oxtails

2 medium yellow or white
onions, chopped

1 head garlic, separated
into cloves, unpeeled

2 ripe tomatoes, skinned
and peeled (see page 17)

2 medium dried red
peppers, finely chopped

2 bay leaves

Sea salt

Black pepper

2 carrots, peeled and thinly
sliced

2 sprigs fresh thyme or
¾ teaspoon dried

1½ cups red wine

Boiling water

SERVES FOUR

*It is said that this dish originated in Córdoba, Andalusia: leather-working and bullfighting country. The leather workers were gifted the tails with the skins they received to work on, and then, as today, there were those that came from the bullfights. Rabo de Toro is now enjoyed throughout Spain and various versions (varying only really with regard to the wine used) exist. This is an easy, super-rich dish that, done well, should be sufficiently gelatinous to stick your lips together. It is properly ready to eat when the meat is coming away from the bone. If there are no oxtails at hand—or if they do not appeal—use another part of the animal (though preferably one with a bone), such as short ribs or shank. This is how they do it at Chikito in Granada.*

*Serve with fried potatoes.*

Gently heat the olive oil in a large pan or casserole with a lid. Add the oxtails, coating the meat well with the oil. Add the onion, garlic, tomatoes, dried peppers, bay leaves, a pinch of salt, and good twist of black pepper. Stir well. When the mixture begins to take color, after 20 minutes or so, add the carrots, the thyme, and the wine. Stir well, raise the heat and let it bubble gently for 15 minutes. Add boiling water to just cover the meat, cover, and cook over very low heat for 1½ hours. Stir every 30 minutes, scraping up any bits that have stuck to the bottom of the pan.

Uncover the pan and cook for 1½ hours more, until the meat is coming off the bone and the cooking liquid has reduced to a few tablespoonfuls of thick reddish brown gravy. Remove the bay leaves and thyme sprigs before serving.

**VARIATIONS:** For a flowerier, yeastier Jerez de la Frontera version of *Rabo de Toro*, substitute 1 cup dry, fino sherry for the red wine.

For a spicier Sevilla version, add one cinnamon stick, half a teaspoon of powdered allspice or nutmeg, and a tablespoon of mixed sweet and hot *pimentón* with the onions, and an ounce or two of brandy just before the wine.

**NOTES:** If there is an excess of fat, let it cool and skim it off; this dish is especially good made the day before and reheated.

Any leftover *Rabo de Toro* (or any beef stew, really) can be used to prepare Basque *pimientos verdes rellenos con carne de rabo* (green peppers stuffed with tail meat). Roast at 350°F for approximately 15 minutes as many green peppers (the small, pointed variety are particularly good) as you have sufficient meat stuffing for. Remove from the oven and when they have cooled, peel them carefully. Leaving them whole, remove their stalks and carefully seed them. Heat up the leftover meat and sauce. Stuff the meat into the peppers and serve sitting in a small pool of the sauce.

# Escudella Barrejada

## CATALAN BOILED MEATS WITH POTATO, CHICKPEAS, RICE, AND CABBAGE

1¹/₄ cups dried white beans

1¹/₄ cups dried chickpeas

1 pig's ear

1 pig's foot (have your butcher split it in half and cut each half into three pieces)

1 beef or veal soup bone

³/₄ pound boneless beef shank, or any stewing beef

1 whole chicken breast, on the bone

1 chicken thigh

1 small savoy cabbage, sliced into pieces ¹/₂-inch thick

2 large white potatoes, peeled and cut into 1¹/₂-inch cubes

¹/₂ cup short-grain rice, preferably Spanish Bomba

2 ounces *fideos*, vermicelli, or angel hair pasta

1 white *butifarra* sausage, or German wurst

1 black *butifarra* sausage, or blood sausage

Sea salt

**SERVES SIX**

*Catalonia's one-pot dinner is a substantial dish, but there's a delicacy to it that is not characteristic of the closely related* potajes *and* pucheros *of the other regions of Spain. This is largely due to the absence of* pimentón-rich chorizo *sausage (a commonplace ingredient in other regions but not a Catalan thing) and to the dish's distinct stages of cooking, with each ingredient being given its own strictly monitored time in the pot so that individual flavors and textures survive and the end result is not an indeterminate stew. The cinnamon- and (not a common ingredient in Spain) white pepper–spiced white* butifarra *sausages are a key ingredient so do your best to find them. (German wurst are probably your best bet if you can't, and you can always add a touch of white pepper and cinnamon separately if you need to.) The cabbage, too, is an important, freshening ingredient and a crisp, not too green savoy will work best.*

*You can always replace the pig's ear and foot with pork belly or bacon. Note that the beans and chickpeas need to be soaked overnight.*

Soak the beans and chickpeas in cold water to cover overnight. Drain and set aside.

Half-fill a very large (12-quart is ideal) pan or stockpot with lightly salted water. Bring to the boil and add the pigs ear, foot, bones, beef, and chicken. Cook over medium heat for 1¹/₂ hours.

Add the cabbage and potatoes. Cook for 20 minutes more.

Add the rice and *fideos*. Cook for 10 minutes more.

Add the sausages. Cook for final 10 minutes.

Discard the soup bones. Salt to taste before serving in large soup bowls.

**NOTE:** *Ternera* (the mild meat of young calves) is used to prepare *Escudella Barrejada*, so for an authentic dish use the mildest beef or veal that you can find.

*This recipe comes from the home of the charming and generous Rosselló family in Palamós, Catalonia, who have taught me many good things about Catalan cuisine (not least, how to prepare it) and something of the Catalan language—which is distinct from Spanish or, as los Rosselló more correctly call it, Castilian—in the process. Escudella means soup in Catalan and Escudella Barrejada means "Mixed Soup" (from the verb barrejar, to mix), and is so called because all the ingredients are eaten together. Escudella i carn d'olla (soup and the meat of the pot) is the same dish but is so named because the escudella and the carn d'olla are eaten as two separate courses, the soup first and then the meat, vegetables, beans, and other ingredients. You can eat the escudella above either way.*

# Pollo al Ajillo

## CHICKEN WITH GARLIC

One 3½-pound chicken
Sea salt
1 heaping tablespoon rice
  or chickpea flour
2 heads garlic, broken into
  cloves, unpeeled
¾ cup olive oil
¾ cup dry sherry

**SERVES FOUR**

*Ardy and Belinda live a healthy, contemplative life just inland from Almería on the dramatically dried-up land that provided the setting for Sergio Leone's* A Fistful of Dollars, For a Few Dollars More, *and so on. The terrain is good for olives and toward the end of every year they deliver those that they shake from the branches of their own 120 or so trees (a mixture of the* picual, arbequina, *and* gordal *varieties) to the local cooperative in Canjayar to be turned into oil. Last year the harvest was a little over 1,000 pounds, which resulted—after the cooperative's cut—in sixty-five quarts of extra virgin olive oil, virgin olive oil, and olive oil (see page 13), enough to comfortably see them through the year. To prepare* Pollo al Ajillo *they use their plain, un-heralded, third-grade olive oil. This is a timeless, favorite southern way with chicken; the yeasty flavor of the sherry goes particularly well with the salt and fried, chewy garlic.*

Wash the chicken in cold water and dry it thoroughly. Cut it apart with a sharp knife or, better still, poultry shears, and then cut each piece into smaller pieces approximately 3 inches square, so you have about twenty pieces in total. Place the pieces of chicken in a large bowl and mix in 1 tablespoon of sea salt and the flour with your hands. Leave the chicken to stand for 15 minutes.

Roughly chop the garlic, leaving the skin on (each clove should be cut into five or six pieces). Heat the olive oil over medium-low heat in a large frying pan or casserole. Add the garlic and cook for approximately 5 minutes, until it is golden. Remove the garlic with a slotted spoon and set it aside.

Add the chicken to the pan, turning it well in the oil. Raise the heat to medium and fry the chicken, turning it every 3 to 4 minutes, for approximately 15 minutes, until it is golden. Remove the chicken from the pan and discard the oil.

Return the chicken to the pan and pour the dry sherry over all, scraping up the bits that have stuck to the bottom of the pan with a wooden spatula. Turn the chicken in the sherry and leave it to bubble for approximately 10 minutes, until the sherry has all but evaporated. Sprinkle with the garlic and serve.

# Sofrit Pagés

## IBIZAN KID, LAMB, CHICKEN, AND POTATOES WITH ALMONDS AND SAFFRON

1 two-pound chicken, cut
  into serving pieces

¹⁄₂ pound lamb (neck is
  commonly used in Ibiza,
  but any cut will work)

¹⁄₂ pound kid (a whole leg
  or shoulder is best)

1¹⁄₂ pounds small white
  potatoes

1 ñora (small dried red
  pepper)

1 tablespoon blanched
  almonds (about 12)

10 threads saffron

1 tablespoon chopped
  parsley

2 heads garlic, unpeeled

¹⁄₂ cup olive oil

2 *butifarra* sausages, or
  any good, coarse pork
  sausages

2 thick slices *sobrasada*
  (optional)

2 bay leaves

1 cinnamon stick

3 whole cloves

Sea salt

**SERVES FOUR TO SIX**

*Ca n'Alfredo in Ibiza Town is delightfully proper in the way that only restaurants in out-of-the-way places now seem able to be: owner Joan Riera doubles as the smoothest of hosts; the service is harmonious; proper place-setting with silver, glasses, etc., is adhered to; the fixtures and fittings are invisibly smart; the wine list manages to be both encyclopedic and thoughtful and the kitchen perfectly practiced. This is the place to discover the food of Ibiza, the most immediately seductive of the Mediterranean Balearic Islands, which also includes Mallorca and Menorca.*

*Sofrit Pagés (as it is known in the Ibizan dialect of Catalan) roughly translates to "Countryman's Fry," but is actually a far more refined, exotic dish than that suggests: the meat and potatoes are braised in a light stock with almonds, saffron, red pepper, garlic, cinnamon, and cloves. You can use pork, lamb, or chicken in place of the kid, and replace the* butifarra *with a sausage of your choice. While* sobrasada *(page 153) is a wholly Balearic ingredient and common to most* sofrit *(naturally, various versions exist), its pimentón content does tend to mask the flavor of the kid and lamb, so do feel free to dispense with it if you so wish. Almonds are not a standard ingredient, but they are included here because they are at Ca n'Alfredo, whose* Sofrit Pagés *is by far the best I have come across.*

*It is a remarked-on curiosity that Sofrit Pagés is one of Spain's most distinct and delicious dishes but remains a relative secret. Eat it as they commonly do on Ibiza, which is for Sunday lunch with some plainly prepared greens or a salad and some fruit and maybe a Caleta (page 150) to follow.*

*Double up on the lamb if you can't get kid.*

Place the chicken, lamb, and kid in a large pot and just cover with water. Bring to a boil and simmer for approximately 25 minutes, until you have a light stock (you will need a touch more than a cup). Remove and set aside the meats and strain the stock into a saucepan.

Meanwhile, boil the potatoes in salted water for approximately 5 minutes. Remove and drain.

Soak the dried red pepper in boiled water for 5 minutes. Drain, seed, and chop fine. Lightly toast the almonds in a dry frying pan with the chopped red pepper for 5 minutes, or until golden brown, adding 10 threads of saffron for the last minute. Mash the almonds, pepper, and saffron together in a mortar with the parsley or combine in a food processor to make a *picada* (thickening powder). Set aside.

Fry the potatoes and garlic in $1/4$ cup of the olive oil over medium heat in the frying pan in which you toasted the almonds for 10 minutes, or until the potatoes are lightly golden. Set aside.

In a large *cazuela* or frying pan big enough to comfortably hold all of the ingredients, gently fry the *butifarra*, *sobrasada*, garlic (this is the second time the heads have been fried), and bay leaves in the remaining $1/4$ cup olive oil for 5 minutes. Add the chicken, lamb and kid, turning them in the oil. After 10 minutes, or when the meat begins to take color, add the potatoes, turning them well in the oil. After 5 minutes remove any excess oil from the pan with a spoon. Skim the stock and heat it. Add the *picada* to the meat and potatoes and combine gently, again turning the meat. Add the cinnamon, cloves, and a pinch of salt and pour on 1 cup of hot stock. Simmer for approximately 30 minutes over low heat, occasionally turning the meat and potatoes so they don't stick, until the meat and potatoes are cooked through, the stock has all but reduced to nothing and the garlic is soft enough to spread. Remove the bay leaves and cinnamon stick before serving.

**NOTE:** If you like a rich *pimentón* flavor but do not have access to *sobrasada*, add a heaping teaspoon of the powdered variety—hot, sweet, or a mixture—with the *picada*.

**NOTE:** On the subject of *sobrasada* and Ibiza, another great Balearic dish is *sobrasada*-stuffed squid, roasted with baby potatoes. If you don't have *sobrasada*, an approximation of finely minced pork or sausage meat with *pimentón* or paprika, salt, and a little lemon zest works well.

# Cordero en Chilindrón

## LAMB WITH RED PEPPERS

8 medium dried red peppers (Spanish *choriceros*, New Mexico, or any medium-to-large dried sweet red peppers)

1 medium white onion, chopped

¹⁄4 cup olive oil

3 cloves garlic, peeled

3 pounds bone-in lamb shoulder, cut into 2-inch pieces

2 tablespoons all-purpose flour

Sea salt

Black pepper

³⁄4 cup dry white wine

¹⁄2 cup lamb stock or light chicken stock

**SERVES FOUR**

*This is a very traditional* chilindrón, *though for an easier, more contemporary version you can substitute skinned fresh red peppers for the dried ones. Whichever way you go about it, the finished sauce should be somewhere between brick and ruby red and be reasonably light, giving a sheen and slight tang to the lamb—and a more mature lamb works best here—rather than swamping it.*

*The recipe comes from Hartza in Pamplona, Navarra, the property of the wonderful and all but inseparable sisters Juana María, Julia, and Manuela Hartza, who surely make it Spain's most individual restaurant as well as one its very best. Hartza takes up the ground floor of a small townhouse opposite the Plaza de Toros (bullfighting ring) in Pamplona and the sisters—Juana María is the maître d' and Julia and Manuela cook—use pretty much only local ingredients, buying their game from local hunters and foraging for other ingredients such as wild asparagus and mushrooms themselves.*

Boil the dried peppers for 20 minutes, or until they are soft. Drain and set them aside to cool.

Cook the onion in 2 tablespoons of the olive oil in a large, deep frying pan or *cazuela* over low heat for 10 minutes, or until it is perfectly soft but not browned. Remove the onion and set aside.

Meanwhile, cut or tear open the peppers, remove the seeds (this is best done with your fingers or by gently rinsing under cold running water) and scrape off the flesh with a knife. Set the flesh aside. Add the 2 remaining tablespoons of olive oil to the pan, raise the heat slightly to medium-low and fry the garlic for 5 minutes, or until lightly golden. Remove the garlic and set aside.

Dust the lamb very lightly with a mixture of 2 tablespoons flour and 1 teaspoon each of salt and black pepper. Add the lamb to the pan, turning it well in the oil, and cook for 5 minutes, or until it is very lightly browned. Add the wine, stirring well. Add the stock and the cooked onion and garlic. Add the flesh of the peppers and leave to bubble gently for approximately 35 minutes, until the lamb is tender.

Pass the sauce through a fine sieve or process before serving if you prefer.

**NOTE:** If you are using fresh peppers, six should be sufficient. Roast them at 400°F for approximately 20 minutes to loosen their skins, leave them to cool. Peel and seed them, cut them into 1-inch strips, and add them to the pot with the wine.

RESTAURANTE
HARTZA

# Fricandó

## BRAISED BEEF WITH WILD MUSHROOMS

1¹/₂ pounds beef shank, boneless and thinly sliced (about ¹/₄ inch thick)

All-purpose flour

3 tablespoons olive oil

1 medium yellow or white onion, finely chopped

2 ripe tomatoes, skinned and seeded (page 17)

³/₄ pound fresh wild mushrooms, or half that amount dried mushrooms, rehydrated

1 cup dry white wine

1 cup beef or veal stock or water

Sea salt

**SERVES FOUR**

*A distinctly earthy and juicy Catalan favorite is this thinly sliced beef shank (cunill in Catalan) with about half the weight in wild mushrooms, braised in white wine and a touch of stock. The Catalans are Spain's most diligent mushroom hunters and this dish is generally prepared from whatever a morning in the woods has rewarded them with. A fricandó should be succulent, and the beef and mushrooms proportionally so. With that in mind, take care not to overcook the beef, and find some fleshy, tasty mushrooms that will properly complement it: moixernons (fairy ring mushrooms) are often used in Catalonia, though porcini work fantastically well and morels take things to another level altogether. Reconstituted dried mushrooms are perfectly acceptable if you do not have access to fresh.*

Dust the beef slices with flour. Fry them very quickly (twenty seconds each side) in the olive oil over medium heat in a large, heavy frying pan or casserole and set aside.

Add the onion to the pan, stir well, and reduce the heat to low. Cook for 10 minutes, or until the onions are soft but not browned. Add the tomatoes to the onions. Stir well and cook for 10 minutes more.

Meanwhile, wipe the mushrooms clean and trim them, retaining the stems only if they are tender. Slice the mushrooms thickly (¹/₄ inch or so). Layer by layer, add the beef slices and mushrooms to the pan.

Pour in the wine and raise the heat to medium until it bubbles. Heat the stock. pour it over, stir well, and lower the heat to medium-low. Simmer for 20 minutes, or until the beef is tender and the sauce thick. Add salt to taste.

**VARIATION:** The Catalans also make a very good *fricandó* with pork and eggplant. With regard to the pork, loin works well. Slice an eggplant to a thickness of a quarter of an inch or so, lightly salt the slices on both sides and leave them to stand for half an hour to draw out the moisture. Remove the salt and subsequent beads of liquid with a clean, dry cloth. Follow the above method but lightly fry (about 2 minutes on each side) the eggplant slices after you have fried the pork.

# Alubias Blancas con Almejas

## WHITE BEANS WITH CLAMS

1 ³/4 cups dried white
  beans or 2 cans, drained
  (reserve ¹/2 cup liquid)
1 small yellow or white
  onion, quartered
1 bay leaf
2 sprigs parsley
2 cloves garlic, unpeeled
  and halved
4 tablespoons olive oil
2 pounds clams
4 blanched almonds
4 threads saffron
¹/2 tablespoon
  breadcrumbs
¹/4 cup white wine
Sea salt
1 tablespoon chopped
  parsley

**SERVES FOUR**

*There is a great, countrywide Spanish tradition of gently stewing together shrimp, clams, squid or cuttlefish with white beans or chickpeas. And it is testament to the quality of their* fabes *beans (see* Fabada, *page 78) as much as their Bay of Biscay clams that* Alubias Blancas con Almejas *is generally considered to be something the northwesterly Asturians do best. However, it cannot be said that the rather rich version of the dish here is wholly typical of Asturias, where apple cider and not wine is the drink of the day and, due to it being the only region of Spain that the Moors failed to conquer, almonds are relatively thin on the ground. For a more traditional, down-to-earth Asturian version, simply remove the almonds and wine and add a teaspoon of* pimentón *or a small, finely chopped dry red pepper to the* picada. *Use the best quality beans you can and cook them as slowly as possible. Alternatively—and more convenient for a quick lunch or supper—use canned beans. Some prefer to take the clams out of the shell before adding them to the beans but they will appear more cheerful if you leave them in.*

Soak the dried beans in water to cover overnight.

Place them in a large pan with the onion, bay leaf, sprigs of parsley, and garlic. Add the olive oil and 1¹/2 quarts water. Bring to the boil, reduce the heat, and simmer slowly, uncovered, for approximately 1¹/2 hours. (If using canned beans, place them with ¹/2 cup of their liquid, the onion, bay leaf, parsley, garlic, olive oil, and water just to cover in a large pan and simmer for 5 minutes.)

Meanwhile, place the clams in a large bowl of salted water.

Make a *picada* (see page 89) by gently toasting the almonds, saffron, and breadcrumbs in a dry frying pan, then crushing them together with a mortar and pestle or in a food processor. Set aside.

Check the beans and add more water if necessary; when they are cooked there should be approximately $1/2$ cup of cooking liquid remaining in the pan.

Gently scrub the clams and drain them. Put the wine and $1/4$ cup water in a large pan with a lid and bring to the boil. Add the clams and place the lid on the pan. When the clams have opened (approximately 3 minutes), strain the cooking liquid into the beans. Add 1 tablespoon of the *picada* to the beans and stir well. Simmer gently for 5 minutes and add the clams, in the shells. Stir the clams into the beans, turn off the heat, cover, and leave to stand for 5 minutes. Remove the parsley sprigs and bay leaf. Add salt to taste, sprinkle with the chopped parsley and serve.

# Chocos con Garbanzos
## CUTTLEFISH WITH CHICKPEAS

2 cuttlefish or squid of approximately ½ pound each

2 cloves garlic, peeled

½ tablespoon blanched almonds (about 6)

1 tablespoon breadcrumbs

3 tablespoons olive oil

1 medium yellow or white onion, chopped

½ green bell pepper, chopped

3 medium tomatoes, skinned and seeded (see page 17)

1 rounded teaspoon sweet or spicy *pimentón* or paprika

3¼ cups cooked chickpeas, rinsed and drained

Sea salt

1 tablespoon chopped parsley

**SERVES FOUR**

*The people of the southern Andalusian coast are passionate about* chocos, *as they call cuttlefish, eating them braised, griddled, or fried on a daily basis, it can seem to the visitor.* Chocos *are rounder and fatter and correspondingly meatier than squid and, indeed, take well to all sorts of cooking. This recipe comes courtesy of Victoria Poyatos, who lives just along the coast from Tarifa, and whose enviable back door opens onto the beach and a view over the Straits of Gibraltar to the Moroccan coast.*

*You can use squid in place of the cuttlefish. And, as with the Shrimp with Chickpeas on page 107, canned chickpeas make this a very quick and easy dish.*

Clean the cuttlefish (see page 11, or have your fishmonger do it for you) and cut them into chunks of approximately 1½ inches square.

Gently heat the garlic and almonds in a large, dry frying pan or *cazuela* for approximately 5 minutes, until both are lightly golden. Add the breadcrumbs, stir well, and transfer to a mortar or food processor to make a *picada* (see page 89) by crushing them together.

Pour the olive oil into the frying pan and heat over low heat. Add the onion to the pan, stirring well. Add the green pepper to the onion. Cook for approximately 15 minutes, until both the onion and pepper are soft but not browned. Stir the tomatoes into the onion and pepper. Stir in the *pimentón*. Cook for 5 minutes. Add the cuttlefish, chickpeas, and a pinch of salt. Add ¾ cup water, stir well, and cook for 10 minutes. Add 1 rounded tablespoon of the *picada* and the chopped parsley, again stir well, and cook for 5 minutes more, until the cuttlefish is tender and easily speared by a fork.

# Gambas con Garbanzos

## SHRIMP WITH CHICKPEAS

*Chickpeas work perfectly here, gradually becoming sweet and so heavy with the tomatoes and juice of the shrimp that they tend to break up. It is essential that you cook the shrimp with their heads on; that is where the flavor that you want is and the other ingredients will all but swamp them and make the dish a touch bland if you don't. Feel free to use whatever you like or have on hand in the* picada *(see page 89); hazelnuts or pine nuts are very good in place of or in addition to the almonds or breadcrumbs. This version uses canned chickpeas, which makes it as easy as it is quick. You will find this dish all along the Mediterranean coast.*

Roll the almonds around in a large, dry frying pan or *cazuela* over low heat for approximately 5 minutes, until they are lightly golden. Finely chop the *ñoras* and add them to the pan with the breadcrumbs. Heat through for 30 seconds and transfer all to a mortar or processor and crush or blend them together to make a *picada*. Set aside.

Heat the olive oil over medium-low heat in the same pan. Add the shrimp and cook for about 15 seconds on each side. Set the shrimp aside.

Add the onion and green pepper to the pan, stirring well. Cook over low heat for approximately 10 minutes, until they are soft but not browned. Add the garlic to the onions and peppers. Add the tomatoes to the pan, stirring well. Cook for 10 minutes. Add the chickpeas. Pour in 3/4 cup water and stir well. Cook for 5 minutes. Add a rounded tablespoon of the *picada*. Stir well and cook for 5 minutes more.

Add the shrimp and cook for 3 minutes, until they are properly warmed through yet still juicy. Add salt to taste. Sprinkle with the chopped parsley and serve.

1/2 tablespoon blanched almonds (about 6)

2 *ñoras* (small, dried red peppers)

1 1/2 teaspoons breadcrumbs

3 tablespoons olive oil

16 large shrimp or 8 langoustine, heads on

1 medium yellow or white onion, chopped

1/2 green bell pepper, seeded and chopped

2 cloves garlic, finely chopped

3 tomatoes, skinned and seeded (page 17)

3 1/4 cups cooked chickpeas, rinsed and drained

Sea salt

1 tablespoon chopped parsley

**SERVES FOUR**

# Solomillo de Cerdo Adobado

## ORANGE AND HONEY MARINATED PORK LOIN

2 cloves garlic, peeled
Juice of 2 oranges
1 tablespoon rosemary
  honey or any good,
  aromatic honey
One 2- to 2½-pound loin
  of pork
Sea salt
Black pepper
1 tablespoon extra virgin
  olive oil

**SERVES FOUR**

*This citrus-sweet roast is equally good hot or cold. It appears here courtesy of the brothers Francisco and Hector López, sommelier and head chef of their fine, family owned and operated restaurant, España, in the Galician town of Lugo. Francisco describes the traditional cuisine of this part of the world as being* sencilla: *simple, natural, and/or unaffected. Note that you will need to marinate the pork for at least six hours before cooking it.*

*This is excellent served either hot with pureed potatoes or cold with a lightly dressed escarole salad.*

Lightly brown the garlic in a dry frying pan. Crush in a mortar and mix together with the orange juice and honey. Season the pork loin with salt and pepper and place it in a dish that is deep enough to hold the marinade. Pour the marinade over the pork. Place in the fridge for six hours, turning the pork loin every hour or so.

Preheat the oven to 350°F. Remove the pork loin from the marinade and place it in a flameproof roasting pan. Rub well with the olive oil and place it in the oven for 15 minutes. Remove from the oven and pour over the marinade. Return the pork to the oven, lower the temperature to 300°F, and cook for 50 minutes more, basting every 25 minutes, until the meat juices run clear. Let the pork stand for 5 minutes on a cutting board while you reduce the marinade by letting it bubble over medium-high heat.

Slice the pork thin and serve it with the marinade spooned over.

**VARIATION:** Pork loin is commonly roasted in Spain but this dish works just as well (even better, perhaps) with any roast such as shoulder or leg.

# Lomo a la Malagueña

## PORK LOIN WITH MÁLAGA WINE AND RAISINS

*Another sweet, fruity pork roast, this time from Málaga. Though a number of wines are now produced in the region of Málaga, the term* Málaga *still applies, as it has since the Renaissance, to a fully sweet wine made from either the moscatel or, a little less commonly, Pedro Ximénez grape. Substitute any sweet wine or sherry if you do not have access to it. Málaga raisins are famously large and fleshy, of a light and intriguingly grainy texture and fully flavored. Again, this dish is equally good hot or cold.*

⌒

Soak the raisins in the wine. Lightly toast the almonds in a dry frying pan over medium heat. Set aside to cool and then split them in half lengthwise. Preheat the oven to 350°F.

Pour the olive oil into the pan in which you toasted the almonds and quickly brown the pork loin over medium heat. Put the pork loin in a roasting pan and, reserving the raisins, pour over the wine. Add the cinnamon. Place in the oven for 25 minutes. Remove from the oven and add the raisins and almonds to the wine, stirring well. Cook for 25 minutes more, until the pork juices run clearly. Add salt and pepper to taste. Let the pork stand for 5 minutes, then slice and spoon over the wine, almonds, and raisins to serve.

¹⁄₃–¹⁄₂ cup raisins (fat Málaga raisins preferably)
1 cup Málaga wine
2 tablespoons blanched almonds (about 24)
2 tablespoons olive oil
One 2- to 2¹⁄₂-pound boneless pork loin, shoulder, or leg
1 cinnamon stick
Sea salt
Black pepper

**SERVES FOUR**

# Marmitako

## TUNA AND POTATO BROTH

3 pounds fish heads (gills removed) and bones, preferably tuna but any nonoily white fish will do

3 medium yellow or white onions, chopped

3 medium tomatoes, skinned and seeded (page 17)

1 head garlic

4 sprigs parsley

4 *choricero* dried peppers, or 1 tablespoon sweet *pimentón* or paprika

2 green bell peppers

3 tablespoons olive oil

1¹⁄₂ pounds white potatoes

6 cups Fish Stock (page 18), or prepared fish stock

1 piece of tuna, 2¹⁄₂ to 3 pounds (white *bonito* is best, but any will do)

Sea salt

**SERVES FOUR TO SIX**

*Another once-prepared-on-board fishermen's dish that is now a national favorite (see* Fideuà, *page 20, and* Gazpachuelo, *page 64). Marmitako is Basque in origin and first appears on menus in June when the white* bonito del norte *("bonito of the north") tuna comes into season in the Bay of Biscay, a moment that is helpfully and rather magically signaled by leaping dolphins. It is imperative that the tuna makes it to the plate juicy. This recipe comes from the Asador Ripa in Bilbao, where they cut the heat just within a minute of adding the tuna to the pot. Delay for much longer and you will end up with a gray impersonation of cardboard.*

*Marmitako is traditionally served unaccompanied, in soup plates. For a simpler version, substitute chunks of tuna steak and use 6 cups prepared fish stock.*

Make a stock by placing the head and bones of the tuna, 1 chopped onion, 1 tomato, the garlic, and the parsley in 2 quarts of water. Bring to a boil, reduce the heat to medium, and cook for 30 to 40 minutes, skimming off any foam that forms on top.

Cut the meat of the tuna into 2-inch cubes.

Boil the *choricero* peppers in water for approximately 10 minutes, until they are soft. Drain and set aside to cool. Cut or tear the *choricero* peppers in half, remove their seeds (rinsing under running water is the easiest way), and carefully scrape off and reserve the flesh. Cook the remaining onions and the green pepper over very low heat in the olive oil until they are soft and very slightly browned. Add the remaining tomatoes to the onion and pepper, stirring well. Peel the potatoes and "crack" pieces directly into the pot by inserting the blade of a knife into them lengthwise to a depth of about ¹⁄₂ inch and gently twisting until they break into $1^1/_2$-inch pieces. Stir the potatoes into the onion, pepper, and tomato mixture. Add the flesh of the *choricero* peppers.

Strain the hot stock and add 6 cups of it or the prepared fish stock ($4^1/_2$ or 5 cups are fine if you do not have more) to the pot. Stir well and simmer for 20 minutes, or until the potatoes are very nearly done. Increase the heat to medium-high for approximately 3 minutes to thicken it. Reduce the heat to low and add the tuna. Add salt to taste. Turn off the heat after 50 seconds and serve immediately.

**NOTE:** "Cracking" the potatoes results in a noticeably thicker broth.

**VARIATION:** *Marmitakos* are also prepared with squid or mackerel.

# Cordero a la Pastoril

## GRANADAN SHEPHERDS' LAMB STEW

3 tablespoons olive oil

2¹⁄₂ pounds breast of
  lamb, cut into 2-inch-
  square pieces

2 medium yellow or white
  onions, chopped

3 cloves garlic, chopped

1 tablespoon all-purpose
  flour

1 tablespoon sweet
  *pimentón* or paprika

3⁄4 cup white wine

2 bay leaves

1 small dried or fresh chile,
  seeded and finely
  chopped

Sea salt

**SERVES FOUR**

The small, rectangular, gray marble–topped tables at the restaurant *Sevilla* in the city of Granada haven't changed since opening day 1930, when the locally born poet Federico García Lorca entertained his friend Salvador Dalí at them. Founded by his great-grandfather, the restaurant is now the property of head chef Dani Álvarez, who likes to experiment a little but still finds a demand for—and room on his menu to offer—a traditional taste of the city and the inland Andalusian province of the same name over which it presides.

This is an easy, deliciously sticky stew. It was originally a shepherds' dish (shepherds vie only with fishermen in being Spain's most prolific inventors of dishes) and this version comes from the hilly north of the province of Granada—true shepherd country—where it is made with the indigenous, slightly gamey Segureño breed of sheep. Lamb, incidentally, was referred to for some time in post-Reconquista Spain (the end of the fifteenth century, when the Catholic kings wrested control of Spain from the Muslim Moors) as "meat of the Arabs."

Heat the olive oil in a *cazuela* or deep frying pan. Add the lamb and stir well to coat with the oil. Add the onion and garlic, stirring well. When the lamb, onion, and garlic begin to take color, add the flour and the *pimentón*, again stirring well. Add the wine. Add the bay leaves. Add the chile. Stir well. Pour in water until it just covers the lamb and cook over low heat, uncovered, stirring occasionally, for 2 hours, or until the lamb is tender and the sauce has reduced to 4 or 5 thick tablespoons. Add salt to taste. Remove the bay leaves before serving.

# Atún Encebollado

## TUNA WITH SWEET ONIONS

*The* almadraba *exists today as it did in Roman times and can be seen from April until August anywhere along the Andalusian coast between the Isla de las Palomas ("Island of the Doves," the marker for where the Mediterranean meets the Atlantic) and Cádiz. A dozen or so boats group together with a maze of nets suspended between them to channel the migrant red tuna, en route to the spawning waters of the Mediterranean, up to the surface to be hooked in by hand. It's a bloody way of doing things.*

*This recipe comes from Spain's wind-surfing capital of Tarifa, a place where the people have attracted an undeserved reputation for speaking to themselves.*

2 tablespoons olive oil

4 tablespoons unsalted butter

2$^1$/$_2$ pounds sweet yellow or white onions, finely chopped

2 cloves garlic, finely chopped

1 cup medium-dry white wine

1 bay leaf

Sea salt

4 thick tuna steaks, approximately 1$^1$/$_2$ pounds

**SERVES FOUR**

Gently heat the olive oil and butter over very low heat in a large, heavy frying pan. Add the onion and garlic to the pan. Stir well to coat the onion thoroughly with the oil and butter. Stirring regularly, cook for 20 minutes, or until the onion is soft and transparent without allowing it to brown. Add the wine and bay leaf, stir well, and continue to cook for another 40 minutes, or until you have something the consistency of a puree. Remove the bay leaf. Add salt to taste.

Preheat the oven to 400°F. Sear the tuna steaks on both sides over high heat in a lightly oiled frying pan or griddle. Place them on a lightly oiled baking dish and cover each with a generous amount of the onion mixture. Place in the oven and cook for 10 minutes, or until the onion mixture begins to brown and crisp.

# Bacalao a la Vizcaína

## SALT COD WITH RED PEPPERS

12 large dried red peppers
(if you can't find Spanish
*choricero*, New Mexico or
any dried sweet peppers
are okay)
1 medium red onion, finely
chopped
3 tablespoons olive oil
2 cloves garlic, finely
chopped
1 medium tomato, skinned
and seeded (see page 17)
1¹⁄₂ pounds desalted salt
cod (see page 16)
1 tablespoon breadcrumbs
1 tablespoon chopped
parsley (optional)

**SERVES FOUR**

*A beautifully bold, blood-red colored dish, the best examples of which appear to have been Chinese lacquered. The color comes from the flesh of rehydrated dried red peppers that are called* choriceros *or, simply,* pimientos de salsa *(sauce peppers). Bacalao a la Vizcaína (Vizcaína being a province of the Basque region) is the Basques' preferred way with salt cod. This recipe was given to me by the aptly named Juana Bilbao, a lovely and generously knowledgeable vendor of fine vegetables—choriceros included—at Bilbao's Mercado de la Ribera. The sauce is judged on the luster of its finish as much as its taste, so if you want to be authentic it is worth the bother of pureeing it in a food processor or at least sieving it at the end. You can use fresh cod or any white fish in place of the salt cod, which, for no apparent reason, is always served skin side up in this dish. Serve with boiled potatoes, white beans, or chickpeas.*

Boil the peppers for approximately 15 minutes, until they are soft. Drain and set aside to cool, retaining the water in which they were boiled.

Cook the onion in the olive oil over very low heat for 10 minutes, or until it is soft but not brown. Add the garlic to the onion. Add the tomato to the onion and garlic, stirring well. Cut or tear the peppers in half, seed them (this is best done with your fingers or by quickly rinsing them under cold running water) and scrape off their flesh with a knife (12 large peppers should give you approximately 4 tablespoons of flesh). Add the flesh of the peppers to the onion and tomato and stir well.

Place the salt cod in a separate pan, cover with the water in which you boiled the peppers, and bring to a boil. Remove the salt cod and set it aside, retaining the water in which you cooked it.

Preheat the oven to 400°F. Add the breadcrumbs and 3 to 4 tablespoons of the water in which the peppers and cod were boiled to the onion mixture. Raise the heat to medium and cook for 5 minutes, stirring well. If you prefer a smooth sauce, transfer the mixture to a food processor and puree it. Spread 4 to 5 tablespoons of the sauce in a *cazuela* or baking dish, place the fish on top, skin side up, and spoon over the rest of the sauce (if you do not have sufficient sauce to cover the fish, thin it slightly by adding more of the water in which the peppers and cod were boiled). Place in the oven for 15 minutes. Sprinkle with chopped parsley.

*Bilbao's Mercado de la Ribera is the largest food market in Spain (though Valencia's Mercado Central makes the same claim . . .) and consists of two floors, each the length and half the width of a U.S. football field. It was built in 1930 in what is called the racionalismo style and from the outside resembles a large, golden yellow, mildly elaborate Spanish colonial railway station. Outside, on the steps up to the main entrance, there sits the customary, black-wrapped Gypsy woman with a basket of garlic and lemons. Inside, the ground floor is all blindingly white tiles and sloping marble tops, thickly spread with all that can be eaten from the Atlantic, all illuminated by miles of double-backed strip lights. Upstairs, there's pork, beef, lamb and kid, poultry, game, vegetables, infinite varieties of dried bean, preserves, fresh and dried fruit, nuts, olives, eggs, cheeses, ham, and cured meats and sausages.*

# Merluza al Albariño

## HAKE WITH SWEET ONIONS, CLAMS, AND ALBARIÑO WINE

24 little neck clams or cockles

4 tablespoons butter (salted or unsalted)

2 tablespoons olive oil, plus extra for the fish

2¹⁄₂ pounds sweet yellow or white onions, chopped

1 clove garlic, finely chopped

1 cup medium-dry white wine (Albariño or something slightly fruity)

4 or 8 (depending on their size) hake steaks, cut across the bone, 1¹⁄₂ to 2 pounds total weight

1 tablespoon chopped parsley

**SERVES FOUR**

*This is from Galicia in the green and wet northwest, though in method and ingredients, it is not a dissimilar dish to the Tuna with Sweet Onions (page 113) from the Andalusian coast at the other end of the country; the only real difference is that here the fish is baked on top of the onions instead of underneath them.*

*Galicia is on the Atlantic and enjoys some of the best fish and shellfish in the world. Inland it produces unbeatable beef, vegetables, white wines (such as the Albariño used here, see Note on opposite page), butter, cream, and soft cheeses. In keeping with the quality of this raw produce, Galician cuisine tends to not be overly elaborate.*

*This recipe comes from the charming Zuñiga Vidal family of the hostal and restaurant La Palma in Vigo, Spain's largest fishing port and a proud, large-scale, granite-built city. Father José and mother América left Galicia for Buenos Aires in 1947, returning with two three-year-old boys, Marcelo and Roberto—who still speak with Argentine accents—on (memorably, for José) 29 March 1972. They took over La Palma, José in the kitchen and América taking care of everything else. Now the roles are performed by Marcelo and Roberto, respectively.*

Place the clams in cold salted water.

Gently heat 2 tablespoons of the butter in a large, heavy pan with the olive oil. Add the onions, stirring well. Add the garlic. Cook over very low heat, stirring regularly, for about 30 minutes, or until the onion is transparent but has not browned. Add the wine, stir well, and cook for 30 minutes more, or until you have something approaching the consistency of a puree. If the onions become too dry, add a little more wine.

Preheat the oven to 400°F. If necessary, drain the onion mixture of excess oil and butter and spread it flat in a large *cazuela* or baking dish. Lightly brush the fish steaks with olive oil and place them on top of the onions. Bake in the oven for 10 minutes.

Drain the clams. Turn the fish steaks, place the clams on top of the onions, and bake for 5 minutes more, until the clams have opened. Sprinkle with the chopped parsley, and serve.

**NOTE:** Albariño is a variety of grape, and the wine it produces goes so well with fish and shellfish that it is commonly known as e*l vino del mar* (the wine of the sea). Some say that Albariño is in fact Riesling, introduced to Galicia hundreds of years ago by German monks following the Camino de Santiago—otherwise known as the Pilgrims' Road—to Santiago de Compostela (see page 147 for the almond-heavy *Torta de Santiago* that was apparently originally produced to feed said pilgrims).

*Poverty, the civil war, and the subsequent, dragging repression of the Franco regime forced so many people to leave Galicia—a good many of them for Argentina—that it became known as "the land of good-byes." But now, in the new, inclusive, European Spain, things have changed and many—one, two, sometimes three generations along—are making the reverse trip. As Henry Kamen writes in* The Disinherited: The Exiles Who Created Spanish Culture, *"The experience of exile, for creative spirits, became almost a need, one that gave them liberty to find a context where they could achieve wholeness. The travail of not-belonging was a way through to discovering where one belonged."*

# Caldereta de Sardinas

## BAKED SARDINES AND POTATOES IN TOMATO SAUCE

2 tablespoons olive oil, plus extra for finishing

2 medium yellow or white onions, sliced ¼-inch thick

2½ pounds white potatoes, peeled and sliced ¼-inch thick

1 green bell pepper, cut into ½-inch strips

1½ pounds tomatoes, or more as needed

2 tablespoons chopped parsley

2 cloves garlic, chopped

½ cup medium-dry white wine (Albariño would be perfect, a Riesling would work well)

8 whole fresh sardines (or 16 if they are small), cleaned

Sea salt

**SERVES FOUR**

*Another Galician baked fish dish. Be they fresh or canned, sardines and tomatoes are always a very good combination. Sincere thanks to Juan Pérez, the nicely self-effacing owner of and sommelier at (a nice combination) the very good La Tacita D'Juan in Santiago de Compostela for letting me know about this.*

Preheat the oven to 350°F. Put the olive oil in a *cazuela, paella* pan, or circular baking dish, the diameter of which is slightly greater than the length of the sardines. Set aside one half of a tomato and skin the rest (see page 17) and set aside half of the tomato pulp.

Place a layer of potatoes in the *cazuela* and cover them with a large spoonful of tomato (remember that you are only going to use half of the tomatoes at this "layering" stage), a few strips of pepper, and a thin layer of onion. Sprinkle with a little chopped parsley and a chopped half-clove of garlic and then repeat the layers until you have used up all of the potatoes, pepper, and onion. Pour in the wine, seal the *cazuela* with aluminum foil and place in the oven for 30 minutes.

Remove the *cazuela* from the oven and remove the foil. Place the sardines on top of potatoes with their tails meeting at the center of the *cazuela*. Place the reserved tomato half in the center of the *cazuela*, cut side down, covering the sardines' tails. Sprinkle with a pinch or two more of chopped parsley and the rest of the garlic. Cover the sardines with the rest of the tomatoes pulp (prepare more if you do not have enough) and return to the oven. Bake uncovered for approximately 20 minutes, until the sardines and potatoes are cooked. Dribble a touch of oil and sprinkle with salt to taste and any remaining parsley before serving.

**NOTE:** Sardines are best cooked on the bone but you can fillet them and take their heads off beforehand if you prefer.

# Jarrete de Buey Estofado al Vino de Albariño
## BEEF SHANK WITH ORANGE AND ALBARIÑO WINE

*Warm with orange and the fruit of the Albariño (see Hake with Sweet Onions, Clams, and Albariño wine, page 116), this is a dish for damp Galician days. Spain is not a big beef-eating country, but Galicia and the Basque Country are its principal producing regions, the only places where the meat is hung for a decent length of time to mature, and aged beef is properly appreciated. Elsewhere, the norm is ternera, "veal" that is actually the meat of calves of between one and two years of age: it's lean, has a mild taste, and is often something of a disappointment to outsiders.*

*Serve this with beans, chickpeas, or potatoes.*

෴

Combine the flour with salt and pepper to taste. Lightly dust the pieces of beef with the seasoned flour and brown on both sides in 3 tablespoons of the olive oil in a heavy frying pan. Remove and place in a deep casserole, setting the frying pan aside. Pour the wine over the beef and bring to a rolling boil. Pour in the beef stock, stir well, and simmer over low heat for approximately 3 hours, until all but 5 to 6 tablespoons of the cooking liquid remain and the beef is tender.

Approximately 30 minutes before the beef is ready, place the pan in which you originally browned the meat over a low heat and add the carrots, onions, and leek. Add the remaining tablespoon oil, if necessary, and stir well. Add the bay leaf and the orange peel. Cook very slowly, stirring frequently so as to not let the vegetables brown, for approximately 15 minutes. When the vegetables begin to soften and take color, add the tomatoes. Cook for 15 minutes more, stirring well. Serve the beef with the sauce spooned over it, and the orange and vegetable mixture on the side.

¼ cup flour
Sea salt
Black pepper
3 pounds beef shank (or knuckle) cut across the bone into 1-inch rounds
3 to 4 tablespoons olive oil
2 cups Albariño wine, (or another slightly fruity white wine of your choice)
4 cups beef stock
3 carrots, finely chopped
2 medium yellow or white onions, finely chopped
1 leek, well-washed and finely chopped
1 bay leaf
Peel of one orange, blanched and finely chopped
2 tomatoes, skinned and seeded (page 17)

**SERVES FOUR**

# Tolosanas

## RED BEANS WITH PORK RIB, CHORIZO, BACON, AND BLOOD SAUSAGE

2¹⁄₂ cups *tolosa* beans, kidney beans, or other red beans
1 medium red onion, peeled
1 carrot
1 leek, well-washed and trimmed
1 green bell pepper, stem removed, seeded
¹⁄₂ pound pork ribs, cut between the bones
1 *chorizo* (soft-cured *casero* cooking *chorizo* is best), about 2 ounces
1 *morcilla* (blood sausage), about 2 ounces
¹⁄₄ pound *tocino* or bacon, in one piece
Sea salt

**SERVES FOUR**

*Tolosanas are tiny red beans from the town of Tolosa in the Guipúzkoa province of the Basque Country. Left to bubble unhurriedly (or* chup chup—*from the verb* chupar, *to suck—as they say in Spain) for a few hours, their flesh turns noticeably sweet and creamy and their already thin skins diaphanous. They are the finest bean of their kind in Spain. This dish is a Basque standard and the recipe here comes from the Asador Ripa (see page 82) in nearby Bilbao. The end result should resemble a thick bean stew rather than a soup. Eat with a spoon and serve with cabbage, parboiled and then quickly sautéed in olive oil with chopped garlic.*

*Note that the beans need to be soaked overnight, and that this is a heavy dish that is only ever eaten at lunchtime and never knowingly slept on.*

Soak the beans overnight in a large lidded pot in twice their volume of water.

Leaving the beans in the water in which they have soaked, add the onion and carrot. Add the leek and the pepper. Add the pork ribs, *chorizo, morcilla,* and *tocino.* Add water until it reaches twice the level of the beans, meat, and vegetables. Bring to a boil and cook at a good, rolling boil for 30 minutes, uncovered. Reduce the heat to very low, cover, and simmer for approximately 2 hours, slightly changing the pot's position over the flame every 30 minutes or so.

Remove the vegetables and either mash them by hand or puree them in a food processor. Gently stir the vegetables back into the beans and cover and simmer for 30 minutes more, until the beans are perfectly soft. Add salt to taste. Slice the meats for serving.

**NOTES:** Different varieties and strains of beans require different cooking times and temperatures and soak up different amounts of water.

Hence dishes such as *Tolosanas* are only truly mastered when you are practiced with the beans you are using. If you are not yet at that stage, do not be afraid to add more water in the cooking if and when needed.

Spain's industrial revolution of the late nineteenth century resulted in a railway line being built to transport coal the long and typically winding distance between León and Bilbao and its iron furnaces. The Basques who manned the train took to cooking their own bean stews on board as they traveled, the drivers and mechanics siphoning off steam from the engine to heat the big three-legged steel and porcelain pots which they invented specially for the job and named *putxeras*. The ticket collectors and guards used the same pots but, being stationed away from the engine, heated them with charcoal. The latter method is still used domestically today, and a *putxera* (the name is applied to both the bean stew and the pot in which it is cooked) festival takes place every October in the Basque town of Balmaseda. The best *putxera* maker (the pot, not the dish) is said to be José Antonio Gómez, a former railway engineer who spends in the region of thirty hours on each example that he produces. Price on application at the town hall.

# Dorada a la Sal

## SALT-BAKED GILT-HEAD BREAM

2 gilt-head bream or sea bass, approximately 2 pounds each (whole, with their heads and scales on)

8 pounds coarse sea salt or kosher salt

**SERVES FOUR**

*A dish from the borderlands of any one of Spain's looming* salinas *(salt flats) which are on the Balearic Islands, the southern Mediterranean coast, and around about Cádiz on the altogether fresher Atlantic. Whole fish are enveloped in a good amount of sea salt and baked. The traditional way is to leave the guts in, but that is only advisable if you know your fish is straight from the sea; better to have your fishmonger clean it through the gills. And do leave the scales on: the salt will draw the juices of the fish toward the surface and the scales serve to seal them in and concentrate them. Serve with french fries or roasted, sliced potatoes (see the recipe for* Ternasco Asado, *or* Roast Lamb, *on page 80), a salad, and a squeeze of lemon. The best way there is to bake a truly fresh fish.*

Preheat the oven to 425°F. Wash and dry the fish. Spread a 1-inch layer of salt across the bottom of a large baking dish or *cazuela*. Place the fish on top of the salt and cover them with the rest of the salt. Press the salt down firmly around the fish with your hands. Bake for 30 minutes.

To serve, crack the top of the salt crust and try to ease it off in one go as though it were a pie crust. Then transfer each whole fish to a large serving plate, scrape off the skin, and, working from the central, fattest point of the flank outward, slide the flesh off the vertebrae with a spatula.

**NOTE:** The slightly glutinous, pearl-shaped cheeks of the fish are widely considered to be the best bits.

# Caldereta de Llagosta

## MENORCAN SPINY LOBSTER STEW

Like most people in the Menorcan fishing village of Fornells, David Coca is engagingly particular about Caldereta de Llagosta. *First, he says, it is as important as it is natural that a complementary pairing of the larger, leaner male and the notably sweeter female spiny lobster be used, the latter supplying the eggs!—which are mashed together with the liver and blood of both to make the all-important thickening and enriching* picada. *Second,* Caldereta de Llagosta *is best eaten gently reheated a day or two after it has been prepared. And finally—and obviously—great care should be taken not to overcook the lobster.*

Mr. Coca is the proprietor of the restaurant Sa Llagosta (The Spiny Lobster), and Fornells is famed for having the best llagostas in Spain. The recipe below, which he uses in his restaurant, was his great-grandfather's and incorporates his grandmother's method for working out how much water to use: two soup-bowlsful of the size you are going to serve per person, plus one for the pot. Fornells has made something of an industry out of Caldereta de Llagosta, and if you intend to visit it is best to do so during the llagosta season, which runs from April to August, as it is a not unpleasant though somewhat dormant place throughout the rest of the year. The picada makes Caldereta de Llagosta a flavorful and surprisingly filling dish and the Menorcans have long eaten it as a solitary main course, served, perhaps, with a dry slice of the island's unsalted, wholemeal bread. The soup and lobster are traditionally eaten as separate courses.

⤙

If you are using live lobsters, first prepare them by holding them face down (keep their claws bound) on a cutting board with their eyes pointing toward you. Take a sharp knife of approximately eight inches and, with the cutting edge of the blade facing you, plunge it into the lobster at the point where the head meets the body. Push down until its point meets the cutting board. Press the knife down and toward you, cutting the head of the lobster in half. Separate the heads from the tails of the

Four 1 to 1½-pound
   lobsters (spiny or
   otherwise, two males and
   two females)
2 tablespoons olive oil
1 medium yellow or white
   onion, chopped
1 small green bell pepper,
   cut into 1 x ¼-inch strips
1 clove garlic, chopped
4 medium tomatoes,
   skinned and seeded (see
   page 17)
1 tablespoon chopped
   parsley
1 slice Menorcan bread or
   dry toast per person, for
   serving

**SERVES FOUR**

*(continued on next page)*

1. Place point of knife —cutting edge facing you where lobster's head meets its body.

2. Press down until point of knife meets surface.

3. Pull blade towards you, so splitting head in half

lobsters and set aside any eggs attached to the tails. Cut the tails into rounds at the joints of the shell. Separate the legs and antennae of the lobsters and set aside. Scoop out the tomalley (liver) and coral from the heads, add it to the eggs, and mash together to make a *picada* (see page 89). Discard the stomach, which you will find on the underside of the lobster, where the head meets the body.

Place the heads, legs, and antennae of the lobsters in a large stock pot and add 6 cups of water. Bring to the boil, skim off any gray scum that forms on top and simmer for approximately 35 minutes, until you have about 4¹/₂ cups of stock.

Meanwhile, in a large *cazuela* or casserole, heat the olive oil over medium-low heat. Add the onion, stirring well. Add the pepper to the onion. Cook for 10 minutes, then add the garlic. Cook for 5 minutes more, or until soft but not browned. Add the tomatoes to the onion and pepper. Add the chopped parsley. Add the tail meat, stirring well. Add the stock, without straining it or removing the lobster heads, legs, and antennae, stir well and bring to a rolling boil. Stir in the *picada*, reduce the heat to medium-low, and simmer for 10 minutes. Leave to cool (preferably, though not essentially, for a minimum of 12 hours).

Gently reheat and serve the broth spooned over a slice of dry, unsalted Menorcan bread (or a piece of dry toast) and then the tail meat.

**VARIATIONS:** At neighboring Can Bourdo they add a hard-boiled egg yolk, four or five toasted almonds, and a dash of *vi ranci* (a not overly sweet, gold-colored wine liqueur) to their *picada*.

Add half a cup of rice with the tomato to make an *arroz caldo*. Or add a "cracked potato" or two (see Tuna and Potato Broth, page 110) at the same point to make what the Menorcans call a *panadera de llagosta*, so called because it was traditionally baked in the baker's oven (a *panadera* is a female baker).

One of the best fish *calderetas* (naturally, there are many versions) I have eaten was at Casa Varela (established 1931) in the city of A Coruña, Galicia. It was prepared with three types of fish—*merluza* (hake), *mero* (grouper), and *rape* (monkfish)—cut across the bone into half-inch rounds, and proportionally sliced potatoes. You can arrive at an easy approximation of it by following the recipe above and substituting 1 ¹⁄₂ pounds or so of each of the fish for the lobsters, making a stock with the heads and a little onion and garlic, adding two or three peeled and sliced white potatoes and a heaping teaspoon of *pimentón* or paprika with the tomato and dispensing with the *picada*. Leave the skin on the fish.

NOTE: One legacy of the British occupation of Menorca of the eighteenth century is that gin is the island's drink of choice. The most popular way of taking it is with bitter lemon, what the Menorcans call a *pomada*.

Gin + Lemon + Glass = Pomada

# Postres

## (DESSERTS)

Arroz con Leche ❦ Tocinillo de Cielo ❦ Torrijas ❦ Leche Frita ❦

Peras en Vino Tinto ❦ Arrope de Castañas ❦ Pestiños ❦ Poleá con Coscorrones ❦

Crema Catalana ❦ Bienmesabe ❦ Higos a la Malagueña ❦ Flaó ❦

Helado de Biscuit con Chocolate ❦ Naranja con Azúcar y Canela ❦

Plátanos de las Canarias Flambeados ❦ Manzanas Asadas ❦

Torta de Santiago ❦ Flan

# Arroz con Leche
## RICE PUDDING

3⁄4 cup short-grain rice,
preferably Spanish
Bomba
3 quarts whole milk
Half a cinnamon stick
2¹⁄₂-inch-long piece of
lemon peel (yellow zest
only, no pith)
Sugar

**SERVES SIX**

*Rice pudding is an altogether big and generous dish and is only made in quantities reflecting that. Remember that it's as good cold from the fridge as it is hot with jam come darker days. The amounts of lemon and cinnamon specified below might appear minimal but to use more would only get in the way of the dish's good and plain calcium-rich starchiness. Rice is an absolute staple throughout Spain and Arroz con Leche—usually topped with a dusting of powdered cinnamon or, as here, burnt sugar—is as much an any-time snack as it is a dessert.*

*This very slow-cooked version (see Variation for a quicker one) is how they do it at Casa Gerardo in the village of Prendes, near Oviedo in north-westerly Asturias, the region in which it is generally considered that Arroz con Leche originated. The recipe was passed on to me by my generous friend Carmen Lligé. The consistency should be that of a very thick soup or velouté and it is worth bearing in mind that the pudding will thicken a touch more while it is cooling.*

Put the rice in a sieve and rinse it under cold running water until the water runs clear.

Put the milk in a large pot with the cinnamon. Add the lemon peel. Slowly bring to a rolling boil and stir in the rice. Reduce the heat to very low and cook, stirring every 20 minutes, for 2 hours.

Add 3⁄4 cup sugar and stir well. Cook for another hour, continuing to stir every 20 minutes. Add more sugar to taste if necessary. Transfer to a single or individual flameproof serving dishes and leave to cool.

Sprinkle sugar over the slightly beige skin that forms on top of the pudding (the sugar will sink if you remove the skin) and burn it to a golden brown with a blowtorch or by putting it under a very hot broiler before serving.

**VARIATION:** For a quicker (a little over three hours quicker) *Arroz con Leche*, wash $^1/_2$ cup of rice as above. Bring 1 quart of milk and 1 cup of heavy cream or crème fraîche to a boil with the cinnamon and lemon peel. Add the rice, stir well, and cook for 25 minutes, stirring continuously. Add $^3/_4$ cup sugar and cook for 15 minutes more, stirring as you go. Serve hot or cold, with or without a sprinkling of powdered cinnamon or lid of burnt sugar.

# Tocinillo de Cielo

## CARAMEL AND CUSTARD

1³⁄4 cups sugar
12 egg yolks
¹⁄2 teaspoon grated lemon zest

**MAKES ABOUT 45 PIECES**

*That this unsparingly sweet, golden yellow dessert is literally named "pig fat from heaven" will tell you all you need to know about the regard in which the Spanish hold the pig. Some say Tocinillo de Cielo originated in the town of Grado in rugged northwestern Asturias, and others say it was invented by nuns in southerly Jerez de la Frontera, Andalusia's sherry capital, to make good use of the mountain of egg yolks that were left over from all the whites used in the sherry-clarifying process. Whatever the case, it is now one of Spain's favorite desserts. A small serving of no more than two or three mouthfuls is the sensible norm.*

Stir the sugar into 1 cup water and make a syrup by cooking over a very low heat for approximately 45 minutes (it is ready when you can make a "thread" with it between your thumb and forefinger or the syrup reaches 223 to 234°F on a candy thermometer). Set the syrup aside.

Preheat the oven to 400°F. Line the bottom of an ovenproof mold approximately 11 × 7 inches with a ¹⁄4-inch layer of the syrup (strain the syrup before you do this if it has started to crystallize). Gently beat the egg yolks and gradually mix in the rest of the syrup and the lemon zest. Pour the egg mixture into the mold. Cover the mold with foil. Place the mold inside a larger baking dish and, to create a water bath, fill the outer dish with boiling water to the level of the egg mixture. Carefully place in the oven and bake for approximately 25 minutes, until the *tocinillo de cielo* is firm. It is ready when a toothpick dipped into it comes out clean. Leave to cool.

Run a knife around the edge of the *tocinillo* to ensure it isn't stuck and then, very quickly, turn it out onto a serving dish. Cut into 1¹⁄4-inch squares and serve.

# Torrijas

## SWEET EGG FRIED BREAD

*Another way with day-old bread (see Garlic Soup, page 54, Gazpacho, page 35, or Salmorejo, page 24), and traditionally prepared—depending on your constitution as much as your geographical situation—with either the humblest red wine or milk. In Castile-León, where they say* Torrijas *originated, it would more likely than not have been wine, while in the relatively grape-free and very slightly more pious northwest it would certainly have been milk. If you are ever in Madrid, you would be remiss to not visit La Casa de las Torrijas (The House of Torrijas) on central Calle Paz (Peace Street), a basic, foursquare, bar-cum-eating-house where little—including the recipe for the obvious speciality of the house—has changed since the thirties. A good torrija is crisp on the outside and soft in the middle and, according to the general consensus, best served hot from the oil.*

1 cup whole milk
$^1\!/_2$ cinnamon stick
One 1-inch length of vanilla pod
$^1\!/_3$ cup sugar
6 large, thick slices of day-old white bread
2 eggs
2 rounded teaspoons cinnamon
6 tablespoons olive oil

**SERVES SIX**

Heat the milk over a medium heat with the cinnamon stick, vanilla, and $4^1\!/_2$ tablespoons of the sugar, stirring well until the sugar dissolves. Lay the bread flat in a large baking dish. When the milk begins to bubble, strain it over the bread, making sure that each slice is properly soaked. Leave for a minimum of 15 minutes (in Madrid it is more usual to leave it in the fridge overnight).

Beat the eggs in a wide bowl. Mix the remainder of the sugar with the powdered cinnamon on a large plate. Heat olive oil to a depth of $^1\!/_4$ inch over medium heat in a large frying pan. Dip both sides of each slice of bread in the sugar and cinnamon and then the egg and fry for approximately $1^1\!/_2$ minutes on each side, until golden brown.

**VARIATION:** For *torrijas de vino*, follow the above instructions but substitute red wine for the milk (the cheapest you can find from Castile-León, if you want to be truly authentic) and do away with the vanilla.

# Leche Frita

## FRIED MILK

3¹⁄₂ tablespoons
   cornstarch
7 tablespoons all-purpose
   flour (3¹⁄₂ tablespoons to
   coat the *Leche Frita*
   before frying)
¹⁄₂ cup sugar
1 quart whole milk
1 cinnamon stick
2 eggs
¹⁄₄ cup olive oil
2 tablespoons butter
Powdered cinnamon

**SERVES FOUR**

*Too many restaurants in Spain pay* Leche Frita *a great disservice, serving up flaccid, off-white, miserably tepid squares of something approaching indistinguishable in taste. It's a great shame because done as it should be, with a firm and hot butter and olive-oil-fried shell encasing a slightly wobbly, cold-from-the-fridge, milk-pudding-like center, it is—as here—a memorable dish. Note that you need to allow at least a few hours for the mixture to stand and set before you fry it.*

Put the cornstarch, 3¹⁄₂ tablespoons of the flour, and the sugar together in a large bowl. Add 1 cup of the milk and mix well with a whisk. Leave to stand for 10 minutes.

Heat the rest of the milk in a large pan with the cinnamon stick over medium-low heat. When the milk begins to bubble, strain it little by little into the sugar and flour mixture, stirring well. Pour the sugar, flour, and milk mixture back into the saucepan and put it over low heat, again stirring well, for 10 minutes.

Lightly oil an 11 × 7-inch ovenproof glass baking dish with olive oil. Pour in the *leche frita* mixture to a depth of ³⁄₄ inch (use two molds if you have sufficient mixture). Leave to cool in the fridge (overnight if you have time).

Run a knife around the edge of the *leche frita* to ensure it's not sticking and very quickly turn it out. Cut it into 2¹⁄₂-inch squares. Beat the eggs. Heat olive oil in a frying pan to a depth approaching ¹⁄₄ inch over medium heat. Add the butter. Dredge each of the squares in the remaining flour, dip in the beaten egg, and fry in the hot oil for approximately 1 minute on each side, until very lightly golden. Sieve over powdered cinnamon and serve hot.

# Peras en Vino Tinto

## PEARS POACHED IN RED WINE

*Small, firm, white-fleshed pears and a light, unremarkable Rioja with—as is often the case—a hint of vanilla to it always seems to work best for this. This is yet another Spanish dessert that features cinnamon, so if you are not a great fan (or are perhaps a little tired of it) feel free to remove it and spice the wine with whatever takes your fancy; pink peppercorns, for example, and star anise are good, and a few threads of saffron interesting. In Spain, Peras en Vino Tinto is a dish traditionally served cold. Peaches and nectarines (unpeeled) are also successfully prepared in the same way.*

4 large or 8 small pears, preferably white and firm-fleshed

2¹⁄₂ tablespoons brown sugar

1 cinnamon stick

One 3-inch-long piece of lemon peel (yellow zest only, no pith)

One 750 ml bottle red wine, preferably Rioja

¹⁄₂ cup port, sweet Málaga wine, or sherry

**SERVES FOUR**

Peel the pears, leaving the stems on. Lay the pears on their sides in a large saucepan. Add the sugar, cinnamon, and lemon peel. Pour the wine over until it covers two-thirds of the pears. Pour on the port. Place the pan over medium-high heat and bring to a rolling boil. Reduce the heat to medium-low and simmer, turning the pears every 10 minutes. After 30 minutes, or when the pears are soft (check them with a tooth-pick), remove them with a slotted spoon and place in a serving bowl. Simmer the wine for approximately 15 minutes more, until it is the consistency of syrup. Pour through a sieve over the pears and leave to cool before serving.

# Arrope de Castañas

## CHESTNUTS AND RED WINE PRESERVES

1 pound chestnuts (fresh are best, but you can use 12 ounces dried—which need to be soaked in water overnight)

½ cup brown sugar

3-inch piece of lemon peel (yellow zest only, no pith)

1 cinnamon stick

One 750 ml bottle red wine (an unspectacular, light Rioja will work well)

**FILLS A 1 QUART JAR**

*This wine* arrope *(they are also and more normally prepared with fruit juice) is prepared in much the same way as the Pears Poached in Red Wine (page 133) but is preserved in jars, to be dipped into throughout the year. There are also fruit versions, with the firm, white-fleshed* piel de sapo *(toad skin) melon being particularly delicious. Pumpkin works very well too. It's not traditionally done, but you might try a spoonful with a slice of a sharp Manchego cheese.*

*If you use dried chestnuts allow approximately 1½ hours cooking time.*

*You'll need to adjust cooking times accordingly if using, for example, melon (approximately 15 minutes if cut into 1½ × 1½-inch chunks) or pumpkin (approximately 30 minutes for pieces of the same size).*

*See the Note on the next page regarding sterilizing jars.*

If you're using fresh chestnuts, shell and prepare them (see page 86).

Put the chestnuts in a large pot. Add the sugar, lemon peel, and cinnamon. Pour in the red wine to cover the chestnuts by 1 inch. Gently bring to a boil over medium-high heat. Reduce the heat to medium-low, and stirring every 15 minutes, let the wine bubble gently for approximately 1 hour, or until the chestnuts are soft but still whole (the wine will reduce by approximately one-third during this process). Transfer the chestnuts to a freshly sterilized jar with a slotted spoon, pour over the still-hot wine to cover, and seal, ensuring the lids are correctly aligned. The *arrope* will keep well for a year or so if refrigerated after opening.

**NOTE:** The simplest way to sterilize jars is to boil them gently—lids included—in water for twenty minutes. Turn them upside down onto a perfectly clean cloth to drain and fill and seal them while they are still hot.

**VARIATION:** As with the *Peras en Vino Tinto*, spice the wine in any way that appeals: one or more bay leaves, peppercorns, thyme, star anise, and orange in place of the lemon are all good ideas.

# Pestiños

## HONEY AND ORANGE PASTRIES

1 orange
1 cup all-purpose flour,
   plus extra for rolling
¼ cup dry to medium-dry
   white wine (a white Rioja
   works well)
2 tablespoons extra virgin
   olive oil
Sea salt
8 tablespoons olive oil (for
   frying)
3 tablespoons honey

**MAKES ABOUT THIRTY**
***PESTIÑOS***

Pestiños *are typically sticky little Spanish pastries. Various versions exist, but this one, from the kitchen of my friend Mari Acosta in Andalusia, is both the best and simplest I have come across. Note that you will need to let the dough stand for two hours before you cut and cook it.*

Pestiños *are traditionally eaten cold but are possibly better hot, with vanilla ice cream.*

Squeeze the orange, retaining a piece of the skin approximately 1 × 3 inches. Mix together the flour, white wine, extra virgin olive oil, 2 tablespoons of the orange juice and a good pinch of salt to make a smooth dough. Add a little more flour if it is overly sticky. Roll into a ball, place in a bowl, cover with a clean cloth and leave to stand for 2 hours.

Heat the olive oil with the orange peel over very low heat in a frying pan for 10 minutes. Meanwhile, cover a work surface with a good dusting of flour and roll out the dough to a thickness of ¼ inch. Cut into strips approximately 1 × 3 inches.

Heat the honey and the remaining orange juice in a medium saucepan over very low heat.

Remove the orange peel from the olive oil and raise the heat to medium. Twist each of the pieces of dough twice, lengthwise, to make a bow-tie shape. Fry them in batches in the hot oil, turning two or three times until lightly golden. Roll them on paper towels to remove any excess oil, quickly turn them in the honey and orange juice, and pile them on a serving plate.

# Poleá con Coscorrones
## MILK PUDDING WITH ANISEED AND CROUTONS

*A sweet, creamy, anise-infused dessert that is sometimes known as* gachas. *It's of southern Andalusian origin and originally took its flavor from* mata-lahúva, *the abundant green aniseed or "sweet grass" that was once cultivated by the Moors but has long since been scattered to all parts by the wind. The olive-oil-fried croutons (*coscorrón, *the name used here for them, also means "a bump on the head") should be tiny and served hot, in absolute contrast to the Poleá, which should come straight from the fridge. The best accompaniment is probably that served by the brothers Calvo at their Méson Astorga in Málaga: a glass of old, approaching black, Pedro Ximénez wine (See Vicente Pérez's Pork with Tomato and the Wines of the Country, page 84).*

5 tablespoons extra virgin olive oil

1 heaping teaspoon *matalahúva* (or aniseed in seed form)

3/4 cup all-purpose flour

1/4 cup sugar

2 tablespoons sweet anisette

1 heaping teaspoon grated lemon zest

1 1/3 cups whole milk

Powdered cinnamon, for decoration

1/2 cup cubed day-old bread

**SERVES FOUR**

Heat 3 tablespoons of the olive oil (reserve two for the croutons) in a deep frying pan over very low heat. Add the *matalahúva* and leave it for 10 minutes to infuse the oil. Remove the pan from the heat and strain the oil through a sieve into a mixing bowl. Gradually add the flour and sugar to the oil, stirring continually. Add the anisette and lemon zest, and mix well until you have a consistent paste. Heat the milk and gradually stir it into the paste until you have a custard. Pour into individual serving dishes and leave to cool in the fridge.

Just before serving, heat the remaining 2 tablespoons of olive oil in a frying pan. Fry the bread cubes until crisp and golden. Drain with a slotted spoon. Serve the *Poleá* cold from the fridge with a sprinkling of cinnamon, if you like, and the hot croutons on top.

# Crema Catalana

## CATALAN CUSTARD

1 lemon
4¼ cups whole milk
1 cinnamon stick
8 egg yolks
¾ cups sugar, plus
  additional for sprinkling
3½ tablespoons
  cornstarch

**SERVES SIX**

*Whether* Crema Catalana *came before crème brûlée or vice versa, and, indeed, where Cambridge cream comes into things are questions that the Catalans, the French, and English have long pondered and occasionally squabbled over. All are sweet custards topped with a crisp burnt sugar lid, and all have their champions. Unsurprisingly, the brilliant and encyclopedic Isidre Gironés of Barcelona's Ca l'Isidre (see Broad Bean and Celery Salad, page 32) puts his native* Crema Catalana *first (it's a Jewish dish that has been around for 2,000 years, he says), though he does pay homage of sorts to Cambridge cream by occasionally featuring that on his menu too. Crème brûlée, says Isidre, is simply a far too rich "bad copy" of* Crema Catalana, *which should be made with whole milk and not cream. In most restaurants,* Crema Catalana *is served in single portion cazuelas, though in Catalan households it traditionally arrives at the table on large dining plates, thus increasing the ratio of burnt sugar to custard. This recipe is that used at Ca l'Isidre, where it is prepared by Nuria, Isidre's daughter, pastry and dessert chef, and heiress.*

～

Carefully take the zest—pith-free—off the lemon in one corkscrew-shaped piece with a potato peeler or sharp knife.

Pour the milk into a large saucepan, add the lemon peel and cinnamon, and bring to a rolling boil.

Meanwhile, using a whisk, beat the egg yolks together with the sugar and cornstarch in a mixing bowl large enough to hold the milk. When the milk begins to boil, quickly take it off the heat and let it subside. Return the milk to the heat and, again, when it begins to boil, remove it and let it subside. Repeat this process once more and then strain the milk through a colander or sieve to remove the lemon peel and cinnamon and gradually add it to the egg yolk mixture, stirring quickly with the whisk as you go. Quickly clean the pan that you originally brought the milk to the boil in, and pour the mixture back into it. Warm through gently over low heat, without allowing it to boil. Pour into the flameproof dishes in which you are going to serve it and let it cool at room temperature.

Before serving, sprinkle with a thin layer (1 or 2 teaspoons) of sugar and brown with a blowtorch or under the broiler.

# Bienmesabe

## ALMOND, CINNAMON, HONEY, AND LEMON CREAM

3⁄4 cup blanched almonds

1⁄4 cup sugar

1⁄2 cup honey

2 tablespoons Canary
Islands Malvasia sweet
wine, or any sweet wine
or sherry

1 heaping teaspoon grated
lemon zest

1 cinnamon stick

2 egg yolks

**SERVES FOUR**

Bienmesabe *translates to an exclamatory "Tastes good to me!" and is an al-mond-heavy, sticky-sweet dessert that quite possibly started life as an Arab sweetmeat (which is also the portion size in which you might be advised to eat it). If served hot from the pan, the consistency should be that of a thick, whisked cream, so dilute it at the end with a little water if necessary. I think it is much better, however, if transferred to a shallow mold and put to cool in the fridge where it sets to something like toffee. For no discernable reason,* Bienmesabe *is particularly popular on the Canary Islands where it is served with cats' tongues cookies (much enjoyed in Spain), either crushed on top as a garnish or whole on the side.*

Lightly toast the almonds over a low heat in a dry frying pan for 5 minutes, until they begin to take color. When they have cooled, grind them finely in a mortar and pestle or food processor.

Bring 1⁄2 cup water to a rolling boil and add the sugar, stirring until it has dissolved. Add the honey, wine, ground almonds, lemon zest, and cinnamon. Reduce the heat to low and stir for approximately 10 minutes, until you have a thick mixture. Remove from the heat. Beat the egg yolks and stir in a tablespoonful of the warm almond mixture. Return the almond mixture to low heat and stir in the egg mixture. Continue to stir for approximately 10 minutes, until the mixture begins to bubble. Remove from the heat, remove the cinnamon stick, pour into individual serving bowls if you are eating it warm or transfer to a shallow mold, place in the fridge for approximately 30 minutes to cool and set, and serve cut into 1-inch pieces.

# Higos a la Malagueña

## FIGS WITH MÁLAGA WINE

*A dessert for a lazy day. You can use any fruit—strawberries, peaches, and melon are especially good—but it possibly works best with late September's sticky, fat-to-splitting figs, a sign of, and a small compensation of sorts for, the end of the summer. You can use any sweet wine, port, or sherry.*

16 figs (black, green or a combination)
2 teaspoons lemon juice
1 tablespoon sugar
½ cup Moscatel wine, or any sweet wine or sherry

**SERVES FOUR**

Wash the figs and quarter them, leaving the skin on. Mix with the lemon juice, sugar, and wine and chill in the fridge for an hour or two before serving.

# Flaó

## IBIZAN MINT CHEESECAKE

**For the pastry**
Sea salt
1 cup all-purpose flour
4 tablespoon extra virgin
  olive oil, plus additional
  for oiling the pan
1 tablespoon anisette
1 heaping teaspoon
  *matalahúva* (aniseeds)

**For the filling**
2 eggs
9 ounces cream cheese
1/2 cup confectioners'
  sugar
16 mint leaves, finely
  chopped
1/2 tablespoon granulated
  sugar

**SERVES SIX**

*Most Ibizan bars, cafés, chiringuitos (page 150), and even the most bare-shelved of off-the-main-track grocery stores have a flaó on the counter to be sold by the slice and dipped in coffee for breakfast, eaten as an anytime snack, or taken home for dessert. A good flaó is of a stiff consistency, lightly and equally flavored by fresh mint and anise, and faintly crunchy with granulated sugar on top. It was traditionally an Easter treat but, as tends to be the modern day way with such seasonal diversions, is now eaten year-round. Matalahúva is a green aniseed that has run wild in Spain and the whole seeds are widely used as a flavoring (see Poleá con Coscorrones, page 137). You can substitute any aniseeds that you have on hand here.*

To make the pastry, add a pinch of salt to the flour and gradually work in the olive oil, 1/4 cup water, the anisette and *matalahúva* with your fingers. Wrap in plastic wrap and leave to stand at room temperature for 2 hours.

Preheat the oven to 350°F.

In a large bowl, beat the eggs and gradually mix in the cream cheese, confectioners' sugar, and mint leaves.

Roll out the pastry. Lightly oil a flan tin approximately 10 inches in diameter with olive oil and line it with the pastry. Add the filling, spreading it evenly, and bake for 45 minutes, or until lightly golden.

Leave to cool, remove from the flan tin and sprinkle with the granulated sugar before serving.

# Helado de Biscuit con Chocolate

## BISCUIT ICE CREAM WITH HOT CHOCOLATE

*There are a healthy number of people in Spain experimenting with chocolate by pairing it with the likes of anchovies and olive oil and sculpting and shaping it into all sorts. Oriol Balaguer and Enric Rovira come immediately to mind, but the trailblazer was the late Antoni Escribà, a contemporary of Antoni Miró's at Barcelona's Llotja School of Arts and Crafts before he went to work in the family pastry shop, turning out such things as full red-cherry-liqueur-filled chocolate lips and, to scale, bitter chocolate stilettos.*

*Here's something that, though rather less intricate and original than Mr. Escribà's creations, is no less indulgent. Chocolate, strangely, is not an everyday dessert feature in Spain. Much more commonly, it is taken as a thick, sweet, drinking chocolate used for dunking* churros *(similar to crullers) or, sometimes, as with this old Catalan standard, as a sauce to go with homemade ice cream. Don't skimp on the quality of your chocolate.*

**For the ice cream**
2 cups heavy cream or
   crème fraîche
6 egg yolks
½ cup sugar

**For the chocolate**
2 cups milk
5 ounces chocolate (70%
   cocoa, ideally), roughly
   grated
½ cup sugar
1 heaping teaspoon
   cornstarch (optional)

**SERVES FOUR TO SIX**

Whisk the cream in a large bowl until it is stiff. In another bowl beat together the egg yolks and sugar until you have a mixture the color of very pale custard. Gradually whisk the cream into the egg yolks and sugar. Transfer to a smaller bowl, if necessary, and freeze. When frozen, beat the mixture by hand or in a food processor, then refreeze. Repeat the process once more.

For the hot chocolate sauce, bring the milk to a simmer. Add the chocolate to the milk, stirring well until it is dissolved. Add the sugar, again stirring well until it is dissolved. Add more chocolate or sugar to taste and, if it needs thickening, gradually stir in the cornstarch while the pot is still on the stove. Leave to cool and serve poured over the ice cream.

*See these Web sites to know more about contemporary Spanish chocolatiers:*
*www.escriba.es*
*www.enricrovira.es*
*www.oriolbalaguer.com*

# Naranja con Azúcar y Canela
## ORANGE WITH SUGAR AND CINNAMON

4 oranges
Sugar
Ground cinnamon

**SERVES FOUR**

*The simplest and most refreshing of desserts and eaten now in Andalusia as it was by the Moors six-hundred-plus years ago.*

Peel and slice the oranges, carefully removing the pith and seeds. Sprinkle with sugar and ground cinnamon to taste. Leave for 20 minutes before serving.

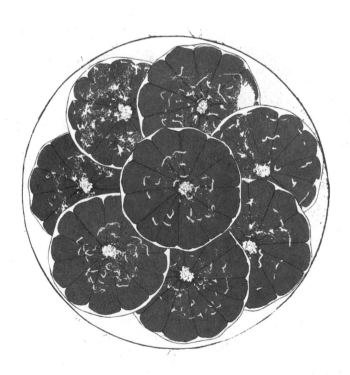

# Plátanos de las Canarias Flambeados

## FLAMBÉED BANANAS

Canary Islands bananas are bananas as they originally were: small, sweet, and creamy, elaborately perfumed, and with unashamedly mottled skins. Indeed, in 1905 one Tomás Zerolo of Tenerife (the largest of the seven Atlantic-bound Canaries) described one thus: "It is sweet with a light acidity, a taste which, combined with the select aroma, is a blend of the American pineapple, the peach and a sense of dissolving firmness." Altogether a more exotic fruit than most of the many tons of bananas now produced in Central America, where it was introduced by the Spanish in the sixteenth century.

The traditional Islands' ways with bananas are to serve them fried with eggs and rice and a tomato sauce (a la cubana) or, as here with their classic contribution to world cuisine, flambéed in brandy.

Flambéed bananas are particularly good with vanilla ice cream.

4 bananas
¹⁄₄ pound butter
2 tablespoons brown sugar
¹⁄₄ cup brandy

**SERVES FOUR**

❧

Cut the bananas in half lengthwise. Heat two large knobs of butter (about 4 tablespoons for 2 bananas) in a large frying pan over medium heat. When the butter begins to foam (but not brown), add two of the bananas to the pan. Turn them quickly to coat them in the butter and then let them sizzle for 30 seconds on each side. Sprinkle with 1 tablespoon brown sugar and turn them again. Cook them for 30 seconds more, turning once. Carefully add 2 tablespoons of brandy to the pan, let it warm, and ignite it either with a match or, if you're cooking with gas, by gently tipping the pan so it touches the flame. Serve when the flame burns out. Repeat the process with the other bananas.

**NOTE:** Sweet, ripe bananas make all the difference with this dish. If yours are not yet at that stage, you could try the Canary Islands trick of wrapping them up in a blanket for a day or so. Alternatively, use a brown paper bag.

**VARIATION:** The Canary Islanders sometimes add a half tablespoon of ground almonds to the sugar.

# Manzanas Asadas
## BAKED APPLES

1/4 pound mixture of any dried fruit and nuts (walnuts, figs, dates, raisins, prunes, etc.)
2 tablespoons honey
4 medium apples
1/2 cup Málaga wine or any sweet wine, sherry, or port
2 tablespoons brown sugar

**SERVES FOUR**

*Golden Delicious apples always take well to baking, but for a taste of the Bierzo region of Castile-León, try crisper, firmer Russets, or* reinetas, *as they call them there.*

～

Heat the oven to 350°F. Coarsely chop the walnuts, figs, raisins, and dates, and bind together with the honey. Slice the tops off the apples to create lids and set aside. Core the apples and stuff with the fruit and nut mixture. Put the tops back on the apples and place them in an baking dish. Pour on the wine, sprinkle over the sugar, cover with aluminum foil, and bake for approximately 40 minutes, until the apples are soft.

# Torta de Santiago
## ALMOND TART

*A heavy, moist tart that is said to have first been baked to sustain pilgrims taking the holy road to Santiago de Compostela in Galicia. Nowadays, it's one of Spain's most commonplace desserts and is usually served with a small glass of sweet Moscatel wine—in Galicia, and in the Galician language, what is sometimes called* vinho de meus amores *(wine of my loves).*

Make the pastry by first beating the egg with 1 tablespoon water and the confectioners' sugar in a large mixing bowl. Add the butter and gradually mix in the flour with your fingers. Add an extra tablespoon of flour if the dough is too sticky. When smooth, wrap in plastic wrap or a plastic bag and place in the fridge for 20 minutes. While the pastry is chilling, preheat the oven to 400°F.

Place the pastry on a floured surface and roll it out thin. Grease a 10-inch tart pan with butter and line it with the pastry.

Finely grind the almonds in a food processor or with a mortar and pestle. Whisk the eggs and gradually beat in the sugar and lemon zest. Gradually add the ground almonds, reserving 1 tablespoon for decoration, and mix well. Spoon the almond mixture into the tart shell and sprinkle with the reserved ground almonds. Bake for approximately 40 minutes, until lightly golden.

Set aside to cool and decorate by placing a template of the cross of Santiago in the center of the tart and sprinkling over confectioners' sugar. Remove the template and serve.

### Pastry
1 egg
1/4 cup confectioners' sugar
4 tablespoons unsalted butter, plus additional for greasing the pan
1 1/2 cups all-purpose flour, plus additional for rolling the dough

### Filling
3 1/2 cups blanched almonds
5 eggs
2 1/2 cups confectioners' sugar
Zest of one lemon, finely grated

**SERVES SIX TO EIGHT**

# Flan

## CARAMEL CUSTARD

1 lemon
2 cups whole milk
¼ cup sugar
2 whole eggs
2 egg yolks
Boiling water

**SERVES FOUR TO SIX**

*Caramel Custard to you and me and, listed alongside a container of plain yogurt, a glass of orange juice, and a piece of fruit, often the only real—as such—dessert to be found on a more basic Menú del Día. Many Spaniards buy* flan *ready-made or as a mix (one of the relatively few prepared foods that they do buy), which is slightly odd considering that it is as easy and quick to prepare with fresh whole milk and eggs as it is good. A couple of strips of lemon peel put to bubble with the milk for ten minutes and a teaspoon of lemon juice in the syrup give this version a fresh flavor of its own. Alternatively, use an orange.*

Preheat the oven to 350°F. Cut two strips of pith-free lemon peel approximately $2^1/_2 \times {}^1/_2$ inches. Add to the milk in a saucepan, bring to a rolling boil, simmer over a low heat for 10 minutes, and set aside.

Meanwhile, make a syrup by melting 2 tablespoons of the sugar over a very low heat and stirring in 1 tablespoon water and 1 teaspoon lemon juice. Pour into a flan mold or round ovenproof dish of approximately 4 cups. Beat the eggs and egg yolks. Add the remaining sugar, beating until creamy. Strain the milk into the egg and sugar mixture, combining well. Pour the mixture into the flan mold and place in a larger ovenproof dish to create a water bath. Cover the flan mold with aluminum foil and pour boiling water into the larger dish to half its depth. Place in the oven for 40 minutes, or until firm. Set aside to cool.

Run a knife around the edge of the mold, and very quickly turn out onto a serving dish.

# Condiments and Miscellany

Caleta ❧ Carajillo ❧ Pan con Tomate ❧ Sobrasada amb Mel ❧
Allioli ❧ Mojo Verde ❧ Mojo Picón

# Caleta

## IBIZAN COFFEE WITH BRANDY, CINNAMON, AND LEMON PEEL

Thumbnail-size chunk of
  pithy lemon peel
Half a cinnamon stick
Sugar
1 shot of brandy
1 espresso-size shot of
  coffee

**SERVES ONE**

Chiringuitos *are beach bars of a wonderfully varying degree of sophistica-tion and a fundamental part of summer living in Spain. And none better represent their true spirit than Sa Punta, which is little more than a bat-tered shed and hodge-podge of the most rickety tables and chairs, all dotted at the most fascinatingly surreal angles, amidst the rocks on the other side of the bay from Ibiza Town. Sa Punta has no electricity and opens and closes with the sun. For lunch there's barbecued fish and squid. But after a late summer swim—and this is a popular swimming spot—local tradition is to take a* Caleta.

*It is said on the island that the* Caleta *was invented at Sa Caleta (which also has very good oven-baked fish and sliced potatoes) in Sant Josep, probably the only one of Ibiza's* chiringuitos *that remains open throughout the year.*

Put the lemon peel, cinnamon, and sugar to taste in a heat proof glass or cup. Gently heat the brandy in a ladle or small pan over a gas flame. Set it alight and pour it into the glass. When the flame dies, add the coffee, stir well, and drink.

**NOTE:** *Caletas* are especially good with a slice of *Flaó* (page 142), Ibiza's delicious, stiff, mint-and-anise-flavored cheese tart.

# Carajillo
## SPIKED COFFEE

*An espresso-size shot of black coffee with the same amount of whatever spirit you fancy. It is still taken as much as a morning reviver as a* digestivo.

⤙

Mix the coffee and brandy together in a large shot glass or small cup. Add sugar to taste.

1 espresso-size shot of
  coffee
1 shot of brandy, whisky, or
  your spirit of choice
Sugar

**SERVES ONE**

# Pan con Tomate

## BREAD WITH TOMATO

2 cloves garlic
4 ripe tomatoes
4 good, thick slices bread
    or toast (sourdough,
    rye—something with
    substance)
Extra virgin olive oil
Sea salt

SERVES FOUR

*In the more rustic of Catalonia's restaurants, a plate of thick-cut bread or toast, properly ripe tomatoes, and a few cloves of unpeeled garlic will arrive at the table, unsolicited, with the menus. Pan con Tomate (or, more correctly, Pa amb Tomaquet in Catalan) is a classic Catalan repast, but so delicious and so easy a combination is it, that it's now found throughout much of Spain. Try it with ham, cheese, or anchovies.*

*The sisters Lolita and Paquita Rexach of the Michelin-starred Hispania restaurant in Arenys de Mar on Catalonia's Costa Brava claim there is no better Pan con Tomate than theirs. They slice their bread (a firm, country bread from the neighboring village of Arenys de Munt) some hours before using it so the cut surface hardens a little and the tomato can take more of a hold during the rubbing process. With regard to the tomatoes, they use de colgar (colgar means to hang), which are tomatoes hung on their vines for some weeks to mature after picking and are small, dimpled, paper-skinned, more orange than red in color, and heavy with tartly sweet juice. The oil they use is an arbequina from Arbeca, the village in the inland Catalan province of Lleida that gave said variety its name when the Duke of Medinaceli introduced olives to it from Palestine in the eighteenth century.*

Cut each clove of garlic (optional but traditional) and each tomato in half. Rub the garlic first, then tomato as much as you care for vigorously on the bread, squeezing the tomato gently to release its juice. Dribble on a little olive oil and sprinkle salt to taste.

# Sobrasada amb Mel

## SOBRASADA ON TOAST WITH HONEY

A good, traditional Mallorcan sobrasada *will come from one of that island's own black pigs that has fed itself silly on figs, carob, and barley. The meat is finely minced and a little sea salt and* pimentón *added before it is stuffed back into the animal's own intestines, previously turned inside out and scrubbed clean with lemon and orange-scented sea water. Then it's hung out to cure in the damp, salty island air.*

*The result is an absurdly rich, soft, workhorse of a sausage that is, among other things, added to sauces and stews, stuffed into squid, fried with eggs, spread plain on bread and, famously, baked with honey on top of toasted* pan de pagés *(country bread) which, in Mallorca, is large and discus-like, unsalted and wholemeal.*

*This isn't a* Menú del Día *dish, per se, but there's a tiny, fussing, black-wrapped old lady at the simplest of al fresco places near Pollença in the north of Mallorca who, come lunchtime, presses a small slice on everyone* para picar *(to pick on) as they arrive.*

⤿

Preheat the oven to 350°F. Lightly toast the bread and spread the *sobrasada* thickly on one side. Squiggle a little honey on top. Bake for 3 minutes.

4 thickish slices of good bread (*pan de pagés* if you can get it, but sourdough, rye, or something with body will do)

½ pound *sobrasada*

2 tablespoons honey

**SERVES FOUR**

*This makes a nice lunch or supper served alongside a tomato salad (page 36).*

# Allioli

## GARLIC SAUCE

8 cloves garlic, peeled
1/2 teaspoon sea salt
1/2 teaspoon lemon juice
    or vinegar (optional)
1 cup extra virgin olive oil

**SERVES FOUR TO SIX**

*There is a restaurant that I forget the name of on the Costa Brava that employs a man solely to make Allioli in the proper, traditional way, which is by crushing cloves of garlic together with a pinch of salt in a mortar and very slowly stirring in olive oil with the pestle (only ever in one direction) until the result is a thick white emulsion. It is slow and painstaking work (this man's working arm is noticeably larger than his other) and an infinitely more difficult job than it appears. That said, if you like garlic, it is also something that is very much worth mastering. Allioli is extremely popular in Catalonia (where it is probably most famously eaten with Arroz Negro, page 52), though it also appears throughout Spain where it is more generally known, in Castilian Spanish (as opposed to Catalan) as ajoaceite. Try it with grilled and barbecued meat and fish. Purists will splutter, but the easy way to make it (see Note below) is in a food processor. Use less garlic if the amount here seems like too much.*

Crush the garlic to a paste in a mortar with the salt. Add the lemon juice or vinegar, if you like. Add the olive oil, 1/2 tablespoon at a time, continuously stirring in the same direction with the pestle until you have something thick and white.

**NOTE:** For an easy *Allioli*, combine the mashed garlic and an egg yolk in a slow-running food processor and gradually dribble in the oil until you have the required consistency.

# Mojo Verde

## CANARY ISLANDS CILANTRO SAUCE

*A distinctly fresh and sharp sauce that is most famously used on the Canary Islands as a dip for* patatas arugadas *(wrinkled potatoes, see Note below), though it is exceptionally good with grilled and barbecued fish, chicken, and rabbit. The best versions are thick and silt-like with fresh cilantro and sometimes parsley. Feel free to adjust the amounts of garlic and vinegar. If you are preparing it with a mortar and pestle as opposed to a blender, take care to chop the cilantro very fine.*

2 cloves garlic, peeled
Sea salt
2 small dried chiles
1/2 teaspoon cumin seed
1 cup extra virgin olive oil
1/3 cup sherry or white wine vinegar
3 heaping tablespoons fresh cilantro, finely chopped

**SERVES FOUR**

Crush the garlic in a mortar or in a food processor with a pinch of salt, the chiles, and the cumin. Add the olive oil and vinegar. Combine well. Add the cilantro. Leave to stand for 10 minutes. Add more vinegar and salt to taste.

NOTE: *Patatas arugadas* (wrinkled potatoes) are the small white potatoes of the Canary Islands cooked whole and unpeeled in sea water. The process draws the moisture out of the potatoes; they emerge firm and almost chewy and without a trace of salt. A rough approximation would be 1 pound of new potatoes slowly boiled with 1/2 cup kosher or sea salt.

# Mojo Picón
## CANARY ISLANDS RED PEPPER SAUCE

1 red bell pepper, or 2
   smaller sweet red
   peppers
2 cloves garlic, peeled
Sea salt
2 small dried chiles
1⁄2 teaspoon cumin seed
1⁄2 tablespoon chopped
   fresh thyme or oregano
   (or 1 teaspoon dried)
1 cup extra virgin olive oil
1⁄3 cup sherry or red or
   white wine vinegar
1⁄2 teaspoon *pimentón* or
   paprika (sweet, hot, or a
   mixture)

**SERVES FOUR**

*The Canary Islands red mojo (see Mojo Verde, page 155) is at its best with the flesh of a red bell or New Mexico pepper or two blended into it, the thicker the better for dipping. Again, this is very good with grilled and barbecued meat and fish, particularly if it's blackened at the edges.*

⌒⌒

Preheat the oven to 350°F. Roast the red pepper for 20 minutes, or until its skin has loosened. Set aside to cool.

Mash the garlic in a mortar or food processor with a pinch of salt, the chiles, cumin, and thyme. Add the olive oil and vinegar. Stir in the *pimentón*. Peel and seed the red pepper and add its flesh to the sauce, combining well until you have a smooth mixture. Leave to stand for 10 minutes. Add more vinegar, salt, and *pimentón* to taste.

# Metric Equivalencies

## Liquid Equivalencies

| U.S. | METRIC |
|------|--------|
| $1/4$ teaspoon | 1.25 milliliters |
| $1/2$ teaspoon | 2.5 milliliters |
| 1 teaspoon | 5 milliliters |
| 1 tablespoon | 15 milliliters |
| 1 fluid ounce | 30 milliliters |
| $1/4$ cup | 60 milliliters |
| $1/3$ cup | 80 milliliters |
| $1/2$ cup | 120 milliliters |
| 1 cup | 240 milliliters |
| 1 pint (2 cups) | 480 milliliters |
| 1 quart (4 cups) | 960 milliliters (.96 liter) |
| 1 gallon (4 quarts) | 3.84 liters |

## Dry Measure Equivalencies

| U.S. | METRIC |
|------|--------|
| 1 ounce (by weight) | 28 grams |
| $1/4$ pound (4 ounces) | 114 grams |
| 1 pound (16 ounces) | 454 grams |
| 2.2 pounds | 1 kilogram (1,000 grams) |

# Oven Temperature Equivalencies

| DESCRIPTION | °FAHRENHEIT | °CELSIUS |
| --- | --- | --- |
| Cool | 200 | 90 |
| Very slow | 250 | 120 |
| Slow | 300–325 | 150–160 |
| Moderately slow | 325–350 | 160–180 |
| Moderate | 350–375 | 180–190 |
| Moderately hot | 375–400 | 190–200 |
| Hot | 400–450 | 200–230 |
| Very hot | 450–500 | 230–260 |

# Resources

ALMAZARA CASERÍO DE LA VIRGEN SL
Camini de Tocón s/n
Alomartes-Yllora 18350 Granada
Spain
Tel. 1-34958340325
The source for Antonio López's organic olive oils.

CHEFSHOP
www.chefshop.com
Tel. (800) 596-0885
Mail order only. Excellent source of all sorts of ingredients including *piquillo* peppers, canned anchovies, and saffron.

DEAN & DELUCA
560 Broadway
New York, NY 10012
www.deandeluca.com
Tel. (800) 221-7714
Mail order and store. *Paella* pans, *paella* rice, *membrillo* (quince paste), cured *serrano* ham, saffron, olive oil, and more. Branches in Washington, D.C.; Napa Valley; Charlotte, North Carolina; and Kansas City, Kansas.

## DESPAÑA BRAND FOODS
86-17 Northern Boulevard
Jackson Heights, NY 11372
www.despanabrandfoods.com
Tel. (888) 779-8617
Mail order and store. Good olive oils, *chorizo*, cured *serrano* ham, *manchego* cheese, salt cod, *pimentón*, and more. Also at 408 Broome Street, New York, NY 10013.

## ETHNIC GROCER
www.ethnicgrocer.com
Tel. (630) 860-1733
Mail order only. Spanish sea salt, capers, canned beans and chickpeas.

## LA ESPAÑOLA
25020 Doble Avenue
Harbor City, CA 90710
www.laespanolameats.com
Tel. (310) 539-0455
Mail order and store. *Cazuela* pans, *morcilla* (blood sausage), salt cod, *sobrasada* sausage, *butifarra* sausage, squid ink.

## LA TIENDA
3601 La Grange Parkway
Toano, VA 23168
www.latienda.com
Tel. (800) 710-4304
Mail order and store. Monday through Friday. Excellent, extensive selection of *olla* cooking pots, earthenware *cazuela* pans, *paella* pans, good quality *iberico* cured ham, Spanish almonds, squid ink, and more.

THE SPANISH TABLE

1426 Western Avenue

Seattle, WA 98101

www.spanishtable.com

Tel. (206) 682-2827

Mail order and store. Exceptionally good wine list, olives, oils, cheeses, pots and pans, and more. Also in Berkeley and Mill Valley, California; and Santa Fe, New Mexico.

ZINGERMAN'S

422 Detroit Street

Ann Arbor, MI 48104

www.zingermans.com

Tel. (888) 636-8162

Mail order and store. *Fideo* noodles, Bomba rice, oil and vinegar, Spanish drinking chocolate.

# Bibliography

Andrews, Colman. *Catalan Cuisine*. London: Grub Street, 1997.

Aris, Pepita. *Spanish Food and Cooking*. London: Lorenz Books, 2005.

Beevor, Antony. *The Spanish Civil War*. London: Cassell Military Paperbacks, 1999.

Canales, Fernando. *Recetas, Trucos y Cantidades en La Cocina Casera*. Camp i Serveis, 2005.

Carpinell, Eladia. *Carmencita o la Buena Cocinera*. Barcelona: Ediciones Librería Universitaria Barcelona, 2001.

Carr, Raymond. *Modern Spain, 1875–1980* Oxford: Oxford Paperbacks, 2001.

Casas, Penelope. *¡Delicioso!* New York: Alfred A. Knopf, 1996.

*Cocina Practica*. Barcelona: Editorial Marin, 1983.

David, Elizabeth. *A Book of Mediterranean Food*. London: Penguin, 1970.

Davidson, Alan. *Mediterranean Seafood*. London: Penguin, 1981.

Deighton, Len. *Action Cook Book*. London: Penguin, 1967.

*España, Parada y Fonda 2004*. Barcelona: Ediciones BCV Reto, 2003.

Facaros, Dana and Michael Pauls. *Spain*. London: Cadogan Guides, 2005.

*Gourmetour 2007*. Madrid: Grupo Gourmets, 2006.

Graves, Tomás. *Bread and Oil*. Totnes, Devon, UK: Prospect, 2000.

Hemingway, Ernest. *Death in the Afternoon*. London: Arrow Books, 1994.

Kamen, Henry. *The Disinherited: The Exiles Who Created Spanish Culture*. London: Allen Lane, 2007.

Lee, Laurie. *As I Walked Out One Midsummer Morning*. London: Penguin, 1971.

Luard, Elisabeth. *Classic Spanish Cooking*. London: MQ Publications, 2006.

Marqués, Quim. *La Cocina de la Barcelona Marinera*. Barcelona: Viena Ediciones, 2004.

Mendel, Janet. *Cooking in Spain*. Málaga: Ediciones Santana, 1997.

Miralles, Boro and Paco Tortosa. *Rutes de Cicloturisme de les Illes Balears*. Palma de Mallorca: Ediciones de Turisme Cultural Illes Balears, 1998.

Ortega, Simone. *1080 Recetas de Cocina*. Madrid: Alianza Editorial, 1972.

Prádanos, Jorge and Pedro Gómez Carrizo. *El Gran Diccionario de Cocina*. Barcelona: RBA Libros, 2003.

Radford, John. *The New Spain*. London: Mitchell Beazley, 1998.

Santos, Rafael García. *Lo Mejor de la Gastronomía 2004*. Barcelona: Ediciones Destino, 2003.

Sans, Pere. *Cuina Catalana*. Barcelona: Editorial Barcanova, 1991.

Tremlett, Giles. *Ghosts of Spain: Travels Through Spain and Its Secret Past*. New York: Walker & Company, 2007.

Webster, Jason. *Duende: A Journey Into the Heart of Flamenco*. New York: Broadway Books, 2003.

Williams, Mark. *The Story of Spain: The Dramatic History of Europe's Most Fascinating Country*. Málaga: Santana Books, 2000.

# Acknowledgments

I would firstly like to thank Marta Calheiros for her patience and understanding and the hugely reassuring enthusiasm with which she took to her unofficial role as chief recipe tester and taster. Special thanks are also due to my agent Anne Edelstein, whose idea this book was, and with whom I share a fascination for Spain and, in particular, the blackboards outside restaurants that advertise the *Menú del Día*. Also, my editor, Sydny Miner, for her guidance, keen recipe checking and, more so, for knowing only too well that food tends to taste better for knowing something about where it comes from and how it came about.

And then there are the following, all of whom have helped in their own way, and to each of whom I am eternally grateful: Mari Acosta; Jorge Aguilera; Dani Álvarez; Juan Pedro and José Alonso; Ardy, Marisol, Blanca, and Marina Amóstegui; Eva Aparicio; Saul Aparicio Hill; Vicente, Martin and Gonzalo Beltrán; Juana Bilbao; Cathy Boirac and everyone at Spain Gourmetour; Carol Burton; Manuel and José Calvo; Diego Casado; David Coca; Javier Deudero; José Luis and Celia Diez; Belinda Eaton; Nathalie Freige; Manuel Giménez; Mari Carmen Gracia; Isidre Gironés; Jayne Hardcastle; Juana María, Julia, and Manuela Hartza; Pedro Hernández; Sam Hodgkin; Jordi Juan; Lisa Kelly; the Knightleys; Francisco and Hector López; Carmen Lligé; Antonio and Marisa López; José Marinez; Katherine McLaughlin; Luis Oruezábal; Sonia Ortega; Jaime de la Peña; Juan Peña; Juan Pérez; Vicente Pérez; Cesar Pesquera; Laura and Victoria Poyatos; Manuel Ribes; Miguel Angel Rodriguez; Pepi Rodriguez; Alfonso Rosselló; Helena Rosselló; Eliot Salkey; Milagros Sánchez; Charlotte Skene-Catling; Antonio Torres; Silvina Torresan; Inés Vilaseca; Jorge Vilaseca; José, América, Marcelo, and Roberto Zuñiga.

# Index

# M

# About the Author

Rohan Daft advises restaurants and retailers on Spanish products. He is a former staff feature writer and gossip columnist on the London *Evening Standard* and has contributed to numerous publications. He divides his time between Andalusia, the north of Spain, and London and has cooked enthusiastically since being presented with a boxed set of the works of Elizabeth David and Len Deighton's *Où est le Garlic?* at the age of twelve.

www.rohandaft.com